BLUESTONE STANDING

BY

JEROLD TOOMEY

RoseDog Books
PITTSBURGH, PENNSYLVANIA 15238

RoseDog Books
585 Alpha Drive, Suite 103
Pittsburgh, PA 15238
Visit our website at *www.rosedogbookstore.com*

ISBN: 978-1-6453-0566-8
eISBN: 978-1-6453-0372-5

BLUESTONE STANDING

BOOK ONE

CHAPTER ONE

The people are not worried. Not on this night of alien mysteries that silences all fire. Women's hearth, hunter, and camps of the hidden have no crackling fire.

This evening, as the dusk bringing retiring sun, paints green-gray illusions across the great expanding plain, the shadows cast are perceptibly unique. Strangely alluring shapes seemingly kissing the edges of the standing bluestones. Mighty blue circles linking the many outlying worlds. None of the naturally meditative people were worried, because so still the night, even the lambs were safe from the blood-hungry wolves. No matter what aggressive kind of hunters of flesh, the calming veil over the forest blankets its wild denizens with a mystical peace under the fragmented blinking skies of ever turning wheels. The cool and murky atmosphere inspires no fires. No need for the safety of ember popping flames on this sacred evening. The wolf lies down with the lamb; embracing as one in the cave bear's den. All aggressions are dampened this night of silent fire.

Having exhaustively danced nature's cooperation, not even the naturally dynamic sky would bring forth her mysterious heat lightning. The moons turned their pale blue fire reflecting faces from the night as if to give passage to the stars appearing with so soft and focused brilliance. The people, mesmerized by the dancing night skies, flew up as one single soul; to the outer rings of life's influence. Soft chants raise these powerful souls high to the place of no worldly memories. In this place of silence, the people could concentrate on the totality of all worlds in the galaxy. They could divide their attention to view everything at once. To respond to any world needing their assistance. From this place come the lesser gods that attend the peoples in need of them. The purveyors of souls who tend those leaving their mortal coils. And too; the redeemer who sits with the High God of heaven and creation. The silent voice within each created intelligence.

The priests worked three months in preparation for the night of silent fires. This was the biggest event in a land impregnated with strange mysteries. To live a fire-less night happens only once in maybe 30 years. It is the time of alignment with stars known only to a few priests working three or four of those years, to predict when the time is perfect. When the blue stones sing. When Lady Crescendjya sings the songs of Blue-stone Standing.

The singer herself; prepared in baths of herbs and minerals deeply heated by orbiting spheres, colorfully pulsing life bringing breath into the sacred waters. The pool; a great bowl of lapis lazuli, gently glowing many iridescent hues, reflecting the memory of the full face of the blue fire sky watchers who are the moons. The waterfall; glistening a green and violet sheen of mystic light, flowing with long splashing tendrils into the vivid twinkling yet calm waters. Cascading streams of brilliant colors caressing and hugging the erotically naked stones as if remorsefully descending into comparative darkness of unknown depths. The spirit nourishing waters falling from some world of splendors, unknown to even these people of singing stone. The moon? The waters? Something opened the petals of the deep purple and bright orange d'vang; the vine of divination. The perfume was so intoxicating only a true bluestone singer could bear it. Breathing it in with every pore. Only a highly trained and talented bluestone singer can allow herself to so willingly blend her spirit with such a dangerously mesmerizing scene. Only she could blend the dancings of the many worlds without getting lost in the complications. Young lithe dancer Crescendjya, adopted daughter of the great chief shaman Almeh, is that stone singer.

Musatta: once a singer, gave way to the many seasons that have stolen her voice. Now, as it has forever been, for the aging ones of this mighty station. Only she serves the beauty of the youthful singer. Assuring the radiant scene is absorbed through the open heart of Crescendjya. Musatta: retired singer, teacher, a wise handmaiden of the young supple initiate, held out the clothes of absorbing for Crescendjya. Musatta's hands knew well the ways of igniting even more sensitivity, more openness to receive the gentle winds of place and time. With strong still delicate fingers, Musatta traced the lines of power on Crescendjya's freshly enlivened, warmed, perfumed, and hypersensitive dripping skin. For the thirty or so year cycle, these ritual baths of the bowed moons cleanse the inward visions of the two women priestesses preparing themselves for the ceremonies of the rings of blue stone. A long sacred path for others to follow. On the night of ascending spirits, the night the blue stones sing, the night of silent fire.

Tra-Aega, the high chief, stood as tall as the staff that precedes his immensity; his eminence. The colorful light spears of his inner man shining brightly from a soul that tenders all things living. Maalsh-aeghai, Tra-aega's mirror spirit, as all married women were known to their men, shone a love on him that would drop a sylvan brute to his knees; as so often it did. These; a people rare, had no war weapons, no need. No army could stand their presence. No warrior, no thief, no dark heart approaching this world could pump a single drop of black blood. The very unmentioned name of this land could bring dramatic transformations. Therefore, the name is ever sealed away from those who would play with the weavings of fate. Only on the night of silent fire are the gates opened to the lesser worlds; the veiled worlds of the struggling material planes. The very reason for the mammoth blue singing stones. The hyphenated names were pronounced as if they were not divided. Such as trayga and Maalshaegai. But they carried a meaning of lineage and station. Others were given single names. Not even the chief shaman carried the hyphenated names of the high authorities.

Tra-aega; as with every such powerful night, stood with the spirit of wisdom on his lips, and the shaman at his side. His eyes lifted to places unseen; unimaginable, for the many who sat before him on the field of the dull, green grasses of dreaming. He looked deep into the past of the ancestors reflected on the faces and souls of the people sitting before him. Tra-aega spoke to Almeh, his chief shaman saying: "Prepare the way for the time is nigh". Almeh retreated to his palatial home to formulate the elixir and incense necessary to purify the long voyagers who would soon traverse the universe. Tra-Aega watched in his mind's eye foreseeing the star boats sailing into the vast frozen. Going only where spirit winds would carry them. This time, to a blue-green planet. A bright blue and green emerald sphere marbled with white puffs of seeming nothingness floating over its firmament. As always, they knew what they came for. They knew an evolving and awakening intelligence was woven into one of the higher evolved animal lives found there. It was he who opened the sky for those of the pearly world an aeon ago. He knew of their need for genetic manipulation. One of the very important purposes of the bluestone circles.

They came to quarry a particular bluestone. Enough to carry home and erect a twin mirroring the one they would erect on the planet as they quarried from the earth of this new evolving world of mankind. Yet another circle of bluestone standing in their ever-expanding plane of intragalactic travels.

CHAPTER TWO

It was a vivid night. The sky was brilliant and the illusion on the land was striking. It seemed the stars came in for a closer look. A blue sheen surrounded the camps of the hunters and gatherers. The people noticed a strange peace that fell on them. Everyone was looking inward. It might have been the shaman's dance. But he danced often, and nothing like this has happened in the past. The people would know because the people remembered everything. They were strong and healthy of mind, body, and spirit. Above the animals, but still, like animals; they lived in fear of their own potentials.

Mosha, the chief shaman, raised his eyes to the stars so close that night. He knew something was different. Mosha checked the crystal he kept in his conical tent. On the dirt floor, next to the centerfire with the flat stone hearth, lay his father's small ceremonial drum; and his own large deer skinned rattle of spirit calling. The rattle was a huge gourd. It was made of the things of the tribal history. Feathers from eagles won in battles with the large birds with talons that could rip apart a rhino's hide. Bones of pterosaurs dangling from the leather wound handle that gave a particular sound like the clacking mating call of the allosaurus. With his ancestors knuckle bones inside to offer their counsel when shaken in a shamanic way. Shaken to the four directions to gather their attention and gain their counsel. He checked the crystal to see if other camps were experiencing the same conditions of this night. His vision was clear and powerful. All people were at peace. Animals were at peace throughout the land. He pondered. He found no meaning and wondered deeply. After all, it was Mosha who held the safety of the people in his hands. Ombram, the chief, stepped into Mosha's tent. He first cleansed his aura with the sweet burning grass. He drank of the bitter spirit water that always sits at the threshold of the shaman's hut. He prepared himself for a conversation with Mosha. Such things are never taken lightly. Nothing concerning the people was a light matter. Survival demanded absolute awareness of everything. Even the night dimmed their eyes vision only a little. Even when the moon hid her face from the earth, the stars offered enough light for a good night's hunting, and a watchful eye.

Deep they went, chanting into each other. In spirit, they walked as one. They walked to the place of dreaming within dreams. They walked into a stone structure of concentric black-stone rings. This is the place where they take unsettled spirits of disturbed people. The circles held them while the people's sheriff dealt with whatever might be the problem. Some were kept forever, some returned to their source of birthing, others were dealt with, corrected and released. None were taken lightly. Tajet, the overseer, the sheriff of the circles was always present. This is who they sought a conference with. From tall powerful Tajet, they sought to learn of the night's strange atmosphere. They only learned the mystery is deep. Wide chested Tajet spoke with the voice of oak trees rubbing their trunks on each other. Deep and moving, with otherworldly authority. He could reach out far beyond the bounds of the mortal world. Tonight, he could not reach. This mystery evaded even he who kept the long record of the people, yet he sensed some forgotten truth that caused him to wonder. They passed smoke and offered prayers to the sky.

Returned now to the people's camp. The two leaders dug deeply into they're minds, trying to say something of value. The people didn't care, they were already in deep peace as if a sedative was carried on the winds.

Mosha took up his father's drum, playing the ancient rhythms, chanting the old songs handed down from the cavern dwellers of early memory. The people went to the place of dreams. It was all Mosha could do. He allowed the people to find their own way through this strange night. No howls from the wilds. No noisome winds blowing. No night birds calling. Even the clicking of the small grass eaters was silenced. No bugs in the air; just a blanket of peace. Mosha shook the rattle of spirit voices and the reply was mysterious as was this night. "Mosha, it is the time of a new age. The stars show a change that not even we can divine". The voice, and the vision, was not clear. Mosha saw only a gray mist that wouldn't give him passage into the mystery time of beginnings. It was tradition to offer smoke to the vision whether or not that vision was clear; he still had to show thanks and gratitude, and so he did with the great patient reverence he was so well known for.

Mosha, done and spent now, as he stood and raised his arms to send the power out to the heavens and over all of the Earth. Mosha froze: the people gaped, the sky was rent open, the stars were gone, replaced with otherworldly wonders. Great ships descended. The people had no concept of ships. They knew not what they saw, yet somehow, they remained peaceful.

CHAPTER THREE

It was the time of demise for the giant mammals. Some still remained. Sloths, pachyderms of a surprising array. Rodents and giant scaled lizards still here from an age ago. Not all dinosaurs died in the great exodus of large beasts. Crocks and giant alligators remained, cave bears and their giant cousins. Saber-toothed lions, and many other things not found in the fossil record. Whatever died was eaten to the bone, very little escaped a belly.

The large mammals dined on each other, they loved their meat. Humans didn't have much to offer, the people were safe from the giant ones. That is if they moved with the flow of things. If they warred, fought each other anywhere, they would draw attention from their carrion-eating friends. Fighting meant death. Death meant easy fixings. And these were not above creating fresh carrion from weakened materials. Many hunting parties fell the animals they hunted. Bears were valued for their lamp burning fat and the medicines gained from their organs. The skin was a wonderfully warm covering in the winter months and hunting and gathering in the high places; the mountains where a night's chill can freeze the giant oryx where it stands and dies.

Energy begets energy. Fighting draws the easily riled wolves and lions from the wilds. Not a healthy emotion, but a great way to draw oneself inward like steam propulsion giving pressure to draw inward, because to express it outwardly is an invitation to death. The people were well practiced at concealing their emotions. Inward is the road to survival in a shamanic society. Inward, yet powerfully connected with others; all things plant or beast. When the inner eye opens, there might be nothing but the people in one's vision. Or, whatever one wishes to see. This gave a great peace, and a false sense of security; the shaman was responsible for the people's safety. He accomplished this through ecstatic dance. The people dance the fire circles around the camp. In their minds, they see the fire. They project that fire around the dancing group. A fire of protection, a fire of connection. Now, they are of one ecstatic mind, one body flowing smoothly as a spirit wind. The shaman joins in and the dance intensifies. Soon, the earth is carrying the low tones of stomping feet into the wilds. Trees are sounding boards that carry tones to the nesting birds and the leaf-eating insects. The earth carries the tones to the deep ground talkers; the giant ones who use their feet as ears on the earth so that they can direct the herd to the watering places, and the mud holes where they get their nutritious minerals. The whole of nature is informed that the people are dancing; the people would soon be in trance. The dwellers of the forest are now at peace; if the dance was true. The shaman holds the safety of the people in his hands. Now, the people can journey to see they're relatives. They can find the herds that feed the people the best. They can now go to the herbal world and learn from the over-mind of the green healing helpers. They could do what they could imagine.

The people survived because they were deeply grounded in the shamanic ways. They knew science well through the labs within their minds. They knew ways to make a variety of machines. Such concepts came naturally, simply by observing the mechanics of nature. These things were not treated wholesale. They were deeply considered, as would be anything that affects the people. They knew machines could change social structure, that could be very dangerous in these times. They could not fight over possessions, so they had to share all things, and own nothing but they're clothes and shamanic tools. The tools such as drums, bones, rattles, and weapons of the hunt were passed down from generations. Clothes were what someone was buried in. When birth was expected, the shaman would make something for the child. He would know before the birth if it was to be a boy or girl. He knows the name, it was he who pronounces the name of welcoming into the world. These gifts became the heirlooms since the time of first memory. Long before the sky opened.

CHAPTER FOUR

From the place of the blackstone circles, where skies are always dark and foreboding. Where clouds of earth-shaking thunder ever threaten in the distance. Where lightning flashes blue narrow channels through a seemingly resistant ether. Never rain, only tangible electric energy stimulates the skin and brings the mind into full awakeness and sharply aware. Still its darkly dreamlike, but so real. Breathing becomes more of a response than a reflex. Each exhale impatiently demands an inhale. Breathing in is an inspiration; a thought, a desire. Exhaling is a prayer; an aspiration, a praise or a willful affirmation. To slow the breathing for meditation requires an enormous effort within the blackstone circles because it is a place of compressed life; a place of deep inward experience. Pain is its threshold because of the enormous willfulness required just to be there. Once calmed; the spirit is prepared for a journey of the great undertaking. The crossing of the unsettled waters that stretch to lands, and peoples, known only to Tajet and the two leaders; Ombram and Mosha. The people had no ships to cross the angry dark immense sea that divides the lands; the continents. Monsters of unimaginable size and terror reside in these oceans. No ships could stand up to the crushing jaws of these leviathanic ocean dwellers. Only over the dark seas could the rain fall in torrential storms of compressed weather, this, because it couldn't stretch its massive black and deep gray clouds over the warmer land. The people could not live on its bright sand shores because of twenty to thirty-foot turtles, and crabs with thirty-foot arms with nine foot claws. Even the leathered long wings stayed away and contented themselves with the delights of the smaller river denizens. They ate of the softer shelled flesh of the spawn of the armor clad ocean fish.

Because of the opening sky, Tajet prepared himself for the journey across the sea. He needed witnesses to the vision, to bring to Etrad and the temple of judgment. He could only undertake this long trek across the unknown expanse in spirit form. Even he wasn't safe from the demons that prey on the lost souls of the dead. Only Etrad had the ability to cross the sea without the special intoxicating herbal protection. But he had to do this because of world law. The shamans of the far lands had to know and be present for things of great importance to the people. So he made an intoxicating herbal tea and smoked of the earth vine with flowers that kill the ordinary people. Even to breathe the perfume would paralyze the unwary. He had to die for three days, only three days allotted for him to be out of his body. First, he had to summon the others who would join him in the crossing of the abyss.

CHAPTER FIVE

The red men of the deep thick forests knew of Tajets coming. They cut the leaves and flowers of their elixir of traveling. Theirs was not so intoxicating as was Tajet's elixir because they would travel on his power; his authority. They had to hide their bodies from the cave bears and cave lions that would surely come for the easy dining, drawn by the smell of unwashed bodies sleeping for three days. No one could know of their hiding places. Because in this land, people were the prey of other people. Monkeys were monsters compared to the fragile flesh of humans. Snakes could swallow an entire hunting party of five or six men. The men hid in secret canyons of the wild mountains. Days journey from the dense forests that protected them from the larger beasts in their busy lives.

Yesh was the leader, the chief, the shaman. Other tribes came to him, no matter how far the journey. Yesh was the keeper of the spells of protection. Others had healers and shamans, but only Yesh had high authority with the spirit realms. He was older than most trees of the forest. Where he came from was unknown even to him. He was shorter than most, but he was expansive of girth and muscle. Yesh could rip the hide off of a waring cave bear. He could, and often did, open and break the jaws of an uncooperative cave lion. He could also speak the spirit languages of the hidden meadow and mountain dwellers. These elvin dwarfs and fairies could easily cast spells on unwary travelers who might cross their domain without giving tribute to them. Travelers felt safe with Yesh. So he led his small party to the canyons of safety. Because of the tight spaces in deep walled rocks, not many creatures would dare the journey into these unforgiving places where food and water were nonexistent.

Soon upon arriving Yesh raised his heavy ironwood staff to the four corners of place and time. He called for the circle of blue-gray mist to rise around and protect the sleeping travelers. The five of them drank of the mix of flower and vine and relaxed into the zone of waiting. Waiting for Tajet to come and lead them across the fearful waters to the black stone circles. The place of meeting. The place where the earth expands its energy tendrils from the center. These tendrils feed the conscience of the mortal intelligence. This is how Yesh knew the exact time of Tajet's coming, as foretold by Etrad.

As Yesh and the three travelers of the thick woods relaxed, they talked of what was to come. Yesh opened the conversation with details of his vision. He spoke of the concentric circles of blackstone. How the circles held people in an inescapable prison, and a place of interrogation; not to punish, but to protect the communities of people, and to hold meetings away from distractions. Yesh had been to the blackstone circles many times before. The world was organized by these meetings. People learned from each other the ways of survival

Shandrill, the house weaver, continued the conversation. He was not a man of fear or unfettered speech. His was the soul of quality considerations. He wove the tree huts from various vines and leaf covered roofs. So tight and thoughtful the weaving, not even small insects could find a path into the protective nest like domes that he constructed in the high trees. To live, or sleep on the ground, was to offer oneself up to the many hungry or bloodthirsty critters. A thick-skinned colorful nine-foot centipede was an unwelcome diner of people. Spiders were none too friendly and were drawn by the smell of sweat. Some could cocoon a full grown man. Leaving him for days screaming, before sinking its mandrills into the flesh to liquefy him. That's if the larger ants didn't claim his fresh meat first. Then, there were the usual, and awful mites and worms that ate into the guts of ill-prepared people. Only by a thick rubbing of the body in sterilized mud could one hope to escape those parasites.

To pass the time of waiting, Shandrill told the story of his mate. Everyone wondered what happened to her, but Shandrill kept his silence mostly. The elixir shut the eyes but opened the mouth. He told of how Meandra was out picking the big orange balls that grew on short trees. Sweet fruit that people love to eat, and flavor other foods with. They ate strange things that no longer exist. Meandra was reaching for an especially bright, ripe ball fruit when a particularly nasty spider bit her arm. Screaming in pain, she ran through the trees to get home. Maybe it was her screaming that attracted the swarm of bees. But only one would've been enough to maim her. A swarm was a rare attack, no one thought she was gathering honey. No one understands why her limp and swollen body was so filled with stinger welts. These pencil sized stingers are not left in the body that was carried and dropped a hundred feet high in the overhang. This overhang was the home of many large insects that fed on rotten leaves and branches. They kept the mid forest healthy. The canopy was another 150 feet above the place of the tee crawlers. No birds nesting in the higher places. The winged ones stayed on the ground and ran down the various antelope, horses, and other fast runners. Too large for practical flight, they used their many-colored feathered wings to aid in maneuvering their hefty bodies. Flapping their wings to lift their weight, to make speed and changing direction an easier thing. The feathers were of dull hues so they didn't stand out and make easy prey for the faster wolf like creatures who hunted in small packs. The larger crawling insects supplement the wolves diet of the smaller and younger birds who were born alive and never through vulnerable eggs. The larger bird parents dined on the wolves.

Most of the land was forest, but it was riddled with meadowed clearings. Further from the shores some deserts were found. The mountains had many regions of forest, meadowlands, and wetlands fed by torrential rivers. These rivers carved canyons; lifeless because of rain inspired flash floods that came too often to support established life. These were the places of hiding for the people who journey in spirit.

Now came Tajet.

CHAPTER SIX

The blue-gray mist of Yesh began a noticeable swirl, much like a small tornado; a wind devil growing ever faster and brighter. As if a floodlight were shining on it, or from within it. And from within this chaos formed a spirit silhouette. Becoming the shape of a tall, perfectly symmetrical man. Two more forms appeared behind Tajet preparing to enter with him. A thunderous voice not unlike rubbing oak tree trunks issued forth: "Make way for the coming of my spirit" resounded throughout the canyons high walls. Shaking loose a barrage of untethered rocks and gravel. Raising a fog of dark matter that surrounded the blue-gray mist of Yesh. This fog dropped its dusty matter to the canyon floor, but the mist remained. The foggy vapers grew tighter around the mist. The mist entered the bodies of the men. Crushing inwards much as the oceans trenches crush the lungs of deep diving whales and other large air breathers. The men in the circles of mist and fog held down the urge to regurgitate; to no avail. The gross matter carried by the bellies present emptied where they sat. Enabling the lifting of the lightened burden of flesh a few feet off the ground. Floating in the air they saw the ever forming man of records and the other two men of the blackstone circles. Tajet had arrived.

A large hand reached out and placed itself on the massive right shoulder of Yesh. Eyes pierced into each other, thoughts and visions were instantly transferred between the two minds that came together; as if knitting a single tapestry of histories deep meaningful lore. Tajet could bring the strange vision of the opening sky to Yesh. Now, the two powerful men were yoked to each other. In this way, they could pull the party along the spirit trail back to the blackstone circles. A path only Tajet knew. A path into the veiled sacred circles of blackstone where the sky was always dark and a black cloud ever rested its threatening and flashing bulk on the horizon.

For the benefit of all. For the benefit of the party of travelers who could now communicate with their respective tribes; the two men, Tajet and Yesh, spoke aloud their shared vision to the people as they slept and dreamed.

Speaking in unison, the two gave an account of what they had shared with each other. It was a strange vibration of unified voices exciting the pineal glands in the minds of the travelers. This done so all of the people who remained behind in the western continent could dream the voices; relaxing the spirits of those who were left behind. Quelling the gossip born of not knowing.

Etrad awoke first, as she was the leader of the tribes when Yesh was off to the hunt, or traveling as he's presently engaged with. Etrad was without a husband, and she coupled with no man or woman. She was married to the timeless voices of the Gods; answering only to them of the high spirit realms. These Gods were the wellspring of the descending waters into Crescendjya's pool of cleansing. Only Etrad could speak with the higher gods. Her voice of authority was above even Yesh;

equal to the voice of Tajet. Her mind followed the journey of the travelers; only she could know of the intrigues; the conversations of the black stone circles. She too was older than the trees. She was the ultimate judge of all the peoples of the earth.

Tajet spoke first. "I know nothing of the rip in the sky. Strange forms descend on us" Yesh considered the words of Tajet. A moment of thought before speaking. "Yes, I have seen the vision that you revealed to me. I have never seen or heard of such things". Now the three men accompanying the leaders heard, but couldn't understand. Never before has such things transpired in living memory. No mode of transportation existed in the worlds of mankind at this time. Water ships had no place in their collective memories. They've watched driftwood float to the shore, but airships were absolutely unimaginable.

CHAPTER SEVEN

It was an awakening vision. The sky with a hole looking into a scene never witnessed before. The outer ring was the normal night sky, often seen and pondered. Through the rip was a vision of colorful stars from an alien world. Far more beautiful and mysterious than what anyone has ever seen. Colors so glorious they blinded the senses. No mortal mind could escape it's wonders. The entire strange stretch of galaxy could be seen with the most glorious hues of lavender, aqua, crimson, deep and light greens all awash in a blue so perfect nothing on earth could compare. This vision reduced around a lensing center showing a solar system of wonderfully marbled planets. In the center the lens reduced even more, there shown a planet of immense size and mystery. It pulls the soul and makes thirsty the desire to float into it. Superimposed against this amazing scene was a ship of construction that baffled the mind. Was it metal? Was it wooden? Maybe stone? No onlooker could say what it was before it melted into a spear of light and landed just far enough from the people that it posed no threat. Again it dissolved into a bright flash that caught everyone's attention as if hypnotized. In its place stood three tall perfect beings. The people fell to the ground with shaking knees. Tra-Aega spoke. So soft and alluring that the people somehow understood his strange language. It was as if he spoke to the soul. "My people, I am here". The people instantly calmed and listened, his voice was a wave of cooling water washing over them. Many creatures, predator and game, gathered and laid in a circle around the newcomers. At peace with the sensation of full bellies, as if they were fresh from a feast. All were calm with ears wide open. All creatures, man and beast understood. Even the flowers and the trees turned their leaves toward Tra-Aega.

Mosha reclaimed his senses first. He spoke with building courage against his shock and fear. "Why? Who are you? Are you the Gods we know in our hearts? Are you the gods seen when the people eat of the ritual mushroom and vines of vision"? Mosha was trying to speak carefully, but even he had no such experience to call on. Mosha, speaking and meditating on the history of the people had no words to offer that would explain this to his people. He also had no need to do so. He instinctively knew this, but he was the people's protector. So he spoke again saying "We bow to no gods, we fear no spirits, we serve only our needs, and the needs of the animals and trees". This he said to ensure his people that he would broker no changes to the tribal ways.

Tra-Aega stared at him and wondered at his courage. Tra-Aega did not know the structure of early earth tribes, he did not yet know these were not warring people who knew nothing of slavery or dominance of any kind. Rare were a people of deeply practiced peace. He reflected on his own world of peace, was this born of necessity, or simply a mutual agreement brought on by past experience? A 'no more blood' bond between the tribes? So, even he considered his words of reply. "We're here to offer what is needed for you and your grandchildren". These words rang deeply within Mosha. Ombram stood by silently listening. A well of respect arose within him for Mosha's fearless speakings. He himself could gather no such courage. His mind was awash with questions he dare not speak. Mosha humbled Ombram. But he is chief and had to show his station. Ombram asked of Tra-Aega; "Then how do you come in flesh and not in spirit as we have become accustomed to"? Tra-Aega peered into Obram who was still trembling inside. Tra-Aega loved Ombram for this and spoke to only him. "We come to aid you, to protect your future, to build on your intelligence". He added, "share this with no one". Of course, this was only a test of Ombram's courage, and need not be obeyed. Loyalty was a given in the presence of Tra-Aega since no evil stood against him. But courage was the test of power in the world of bluestone. Through courage, people gained power and influence in his world. Mosha, having spoken first, already demonstrated his strength. Both men were found worthy of Tra-Aega's love.

Tra-Aega had a second son; Eno-Tra. He now called on him and spoke to Eno-Tra's mind saying: "It is time for you to go and seek the blackstone circles of your brother Tajet-tra". Adding "Tell him his full name, and reveal yourself as his brother he knows himself only as Tajet, so tell him of the family name and heritage and how the names work". Eno-Tra was bewildered, not knowing his brother, or that he even had one. But he gathered his senses, and himself, he then reached out to find the astral trail to the circles of blackstone; to his newly discovered brother. He then vanished in a light gray mist.

CHAPTER EIGHT

The storms the travelers encountered were unusually fierce; even for the big waves of the dark wild ocean. It seemed to Yesh that the forces of nature were in angst over the mission of the travelers. Tejet knew what caused these howling winds; it was born of the peace that descended on the people of the eastern continent; the land of huge lizards and giant mammals. The calm pushed against the trade winds, causing storms over the oceans. The men were safe from the storms; because they were flesh cloaked in spirit. Yet, this storm spoke of something else; something beyond his knowing, and it worried him deeply. He wondered if this had to do with the black clouds on the horizon of the blackstone circles?

It was only a stretched instant from the canyon to the circles. To the travelers, it seemed like hours while passing over the ocean that divides the continents. Many sights were noticed. Whales, dolphin-like swimmers and finned flyers; all large and fierce. They saw eight armed beings reaching forty feet into the sky to pull down unlucky birds with fifty foot wingspans. Long serpents with large heads bobbing. Schools of armored fish roiling across the sea. A long-necked head rising up to gulp a flying leather winged monster; with the back of its head as prominently pointed as was its beak. A school of salmon like fish swimming by in a graceful show of aquatics, only to disappear into a gaping mouth that rose up in their path. The men wanted nothing to do with ocean travel after seeing these things. They understood now why the leaders wouldn't allow the building of sea floating craft. They knew it was possible, but now they know why it isn't done. No matter the desire for fish. But the black stone circle was the only thing in the eyes of Tajet. He was long accustomed to the sights of the sea. He had to follow his vision with no distractions. He was following the astral trail he made when coming to the western continent.

A shore emerged on the horizon. The crashing waves were dwarfed by the huge life forms moving across the dark gray sand beach. Passing quickly over the land of wonders, a gray ghostly mist was seen, and they headed straight into it. The blackstone circles revealed themselves, and there they softly landed. The men gathered into the center circle around Tajet. There were rows of standing stones they could use as seats to choose from. Tajet stood and allowed them to sit around him. The distant storm trembled and issued a deafening rolling thunder that shook loose and exposed any fear among the group. Tajet thanked the sky with a voice that matched the thunder. They were now safely home, and fear left the men.

Spandrel peered into the enveloping mist and swore he saw a form. It was Meandra: his dead wife. He rose to greet her. She approached him and cried in unspeakable relief. They em-braced. Tajet spoke saying "Here, the passing spirits gather. The love of you shines brighter than death. Cherish this meet-ing until you're joined again". Tajet formed a mist for them to enter and be alone with each other.

The house weaver spoke to Tajet; "These wonders I will cherish forever". Tajet replied "Spandrel, you will have many moments to cherish". He added; "Yours is to be a long life". Spandrel: already advanced in age, wondered at these words, but he kept his peace.

Now, it was Tajet's turn to peer into the unyielding void. What now manifests? A man as tall and strong as himself stepped out of a mist and into the circle of blackstone. Tajet knew him, but he didn't know him. This confused Tajet who was never befuddled before the sky opened. "Hale Tajet-Tra, for I have come with glad tidings". Tajet-Tra? Tajet wondered at these words. Tajet knew nothing of his own origins. "Who is this that mirrors myself? Come stranger, and we will speak of your mysterious words. Know you not who I am, how is it you address me as such? Introduce yourself, and know you're in the circles of truth saying. I am only named Tajet, truths keeper. I am the balance between light and dark it is I who allows no advantage to either dark or light, good or evil. I am sheriff of the world of man. Yet you address me as Tajet-tra; what is this truth you speak"? The two stared deeply into each other, and it bore an odd comfort for both of them.

Long was the conversation between the two of Tra. Tra is the surname of the male-children of Tra-Aega. The name Aega is given to the woman children of Tra-Aega. Such was the naming of children of the keepers of bluestone.

CHAPTER NINE

She sweated; she worked, she worried through it all. Etrad mixed the potion of clear seeing: not that seeing was a problem for her because seeing is a matter of levels. The easiest for her visions was a daily duty. Sometimes she had to peer deeper into the dramas of the people. If what she saw was off course with the tribes, it was Etrad who brought forth judgment that none dare disobey. Etrad was older than the trees: older than Tajet, at least that's how she saw it. But neither one knew their own true age; their own true beginnings.

What she saw was a new future; a future that brought her to her knees with terror. But it was nothing near the sheer dread she saw beyond that future. The elixir was unusually powerful; as was the long-hidden crystal she divined through. It was easy for her to follow Yesh; to see the coming of Tajet, to see the travels and the blackstone circles. She shared with delight the visions of the open sea. She saw even through the mist where Spandrel and Meandra coupled. Etrad looked away: feeling it wasn't right to voy, to watch, to remain. She turned her sight toward Eno-Tra and Tajet-Tra, wondering at Eno-Tra's words. She knew he had no choice but to speak the truth in the blackstone circles, and she didn't know that he had no choice but to speak truth no matter where he was. So intense were her studies of the two men, Tajet-Tra felt her presence. He sent a warm welcome to the distant mind of his longtime friend. Tajet didn't know she is his sister until Eno-Tra renamed her Etrad-Aega. Etrad smiled: her heart smiled. She knew Eno-Tra named her his sister and sister of Tajet-Tra. Now she, at last, knew herself. Tajet-Tra's younger sister and nothing could be found more pleasing to her. She wanted to leave the circles of this vision, and weep the women's tears of love and relief. So filled was her heart. Tra-Aega revealed this to Eno-Tra when he revealed his brother Tajet-Tra. Such were the ways of the people who embraced all others. Because of working with all others through the bluestone; all things revealed in their own time. Tra-Aega did not reveal everything yet.

Eno-Tra told his newly found brother Tajet-Tra to leave and visit the people: to meet his father. Eno-Tra was well equipped to keep the circles of truth. Yesh and Spandrel were at peace with this new development, but the other two, The brothers Tiptil and Homa worried between themselves. They kept silent and observed all things. They were the witnesses, the eyes and ears for Etrad's visions. She could do well for herself, but they brought clarity and detail for Etrad. They remembered everything; they were her sons and of no father. Seeing eyes and listening ears go both ways; if the source allows. They felt Etrad's worries, but she kept them from the details of earth's future vision.

Tra-Aega brought change; and change was dangerous. Etrad-Aega knew it was time for a change. The clock of the universe ticked a new age; nay, a new aeon fraught with new wonders, and delights, and new terrors. She knew her time was ending. Because Eno-Tra revealed who she was, she saw how she came to be on Earth. She realized that she came to earth an aeon ago; the first time the sky opened and the first time humans were awoken from their primitive form. It was the bluestone people who changed the genetics of the primates into the various human forms. This time was when homo erectus and homo sapien walked the earth together with Neanderthal and many other species of humanoid.

CHAPTER TEN

Returning, after so many years away brings memories and shock. In a time when nothing changes, the feelings of comfort and familiarity should still be there. Not so for Tajet-Tra. His first vision, after being away so long, was not what he expected. He did expect to greet his father for the first time. He was strong and had no apprehensions. He was calm and expected to greet his father much the same as he and Eno-Tra had greeted. After all Tajet-Tra knew he had a father and mother somewhere and fully expected to meet them someday. But from a hole in the sky was a different matter altogether. These beings were composed of light, not flesh. The tallest of them was flashing brilliant white rays from his eyes, and staring directly into Tajet-Tra's eyes. Never before in all of his time did Tajet-Tra feel so diminished: humbled, forced to the inside. But inside is where they went. It is true that these shamanic people often visited the world from within themselves. But this went so much deeper; to the point of conception. The two of them went to where the sperm meets the egg. Tra-Aega brought his son into his most primal beginnings, and reworked the division of cells into a perfect form. Tajet-Tra felt an electric tickling sensation throughout his physical being. What he felt in his souls he could not describe; except to say he felt forged. Tra-Aega was reprogramming his son's body and mind. He was awakening the ancient cellular memories of the people of bluestone. Tra-Aega moved through his son's mind and memories, he saw the motivations that drove Tajet-Tra to serve the people exclusive of himself. He saw through his son the bond between Tajet-Tra and his sister Etrad-Aega. Any keeper of the blackstone circles is like a sheriff with a woman as a judge. In this case that judge was his sister. It did not have to be this way. Tra-Aega saw the bonding of the two and found it pleasing.

Sheriff in one land; a judge in the other land. This is how the people have linked; anywhere in the world. She, the judge, held her place for millennium. He, the sheriff, went about the world in spirit, and in the body when necessary. It was for the judge to build the temple of power that she would live her entire life in. She too could travel in her mind's eye, and witness the things she would ultimately bear the weight of judgment for; or against. She was the arbitrator of personal disagreements and decided social order. He was the keeper of the blackstone circles that housed the jail where undisciplined souls were kept. At this time, the outermost circles of confinement were empty. In fact it was rare that more than two or three were kept there for any length of time. This was the holding place of co-conspirators. The circles closer to the center were for crimes against the people or environment. The outer circle held those accused of misdemeanors and were quickly exposed and released in shame back to their people. They were tasked to re-establish trust, which meant a long span of dutiful servitude. The innermost circles were for those of a criminal mind; rebellious, vindictive, and jealous crimes of passion. Theft was as unknown as was murder. A jealous heart was someone who played tricks on his victim. Because these things brought out hot emotions that might draw the flesh eaters from the wilds. The people were still primitive, and they lived in a primitive land.

Tra-Aega and his son uncoupled their minds. Tajet-Tra was now a being of light. The two of them looked at each other with new eyes and new wonder. Tajet-Tra no longer felt supreme in the presence of the people. He didn't know anything of his new station or who he was in regard to people. He knew he was on a new path but to where? To what?

• • • • •

Mosha and Ombram were silent and awe-struck at the sight they just witnessed. The transformation of Tajet-Tra wasn't something they had the capacity to understand. Mosha knew him as only Tajet and couldn't grasp the change he just saw happen to someone he knew for most of his lifetime. He felt as empty as someone who lost a friend. He wasn't sure of where he stood with this new Tajet-Tra. So he clumsily probed. He said to Tajet-Tra: "how will you tend to your station, your art of probing, at the stones now? Will you still be there? Do I take my people in need of you to the blackstone circles"? Tajet-Tra for once had no answer to such a common question. He looked at his father with begging eyes; begging for an answer to offer his people. Tra-Aega smiled. "No, you will move on and your brother Eno-Tra will stay in your stead. The time for a new age of man is at hand, and we will erect the Bluestone Standing for the people of Earth. Then we will leave, and then you will understand".

"What of my sister"? Tajet-Tra loved Etrad-Aega and loved her even more now that he knew who she was.

"She will stay and judge for Eno-Tra until this age ends. Unlike you, she is only older than the trees, I have only one daughter, and none can replace her before the next time the sky opens". Being kindly and all inclusive as his nature is, he added, "Ombram and Mosha will make endless bonds with your brother Eno-Tra and it will be for them as if you never left, and they will love him as they loved you". He considered further and said, "your sister will be content to learn the love of Eno-Tra in your stead. You will still be in the lives of your brother and sister and share many dramas until the new aeon ends". Tajet-Tra smiled so deeply tears escaped from his eyes.

CHAPTER ELEVEN

He is as wise as he is large. Tra-Aega knew but didn't say to either of his sons what they should expect upon the arrival of Eno-Tra at the blackstone circle. Neither Tajet-Tra nor Eno-Tra was told in advance how it would go. If Tra-Aega let on what they should expect, their father foresaw how the first meeting of the two sons would take on a whole different path. He wanted them to meet without prejudice; without preconceptions or nervous expectations. He wanted his sons to greet each other with a pure heart and an open mind. With arms of acceptance holding no plans between their first embrace. Only bonding was acceptable at this point. Tra-Aega knew that Eno-Tra had to start fresh and learn from the bottom up how to sheriff the tribes of mankind. He had to learn from his sister judge, and not from his brother because the age was changing now.

Tra-Aega is a deity; as are all of the bluestone people. But only Tra-Aega knows this. To the others; it's just the way life goes. The father kept this secret from the others because he didn't want ego's blessings. He, and his people were servants to a higher mystery. Tra-Aega knew he was only a gatekeeper and weaver of ways within this galaxy. He knew he would be there

when the light bringer rebelles and falls with the host of ego-
dominated angels. He wanted no part in the rebellion, he humbled himself at the throne of the High God, so he was given the
lordship over the tribes of man, and the many other intelli-
gences within the solar systems of the milky way. He held all of
the tribes of the manifested planes within himself. He mirrored
the High God who held sway among all of the galaxies of the
universe. So to say he only had two sons and one daughter applied only to the earth tribes. In fact his progeny was uncount-
able; three for each and every world with intelligent beings in
the galaxy, and a lineage of singers for every circle of Bluestone
Standing. He was aware of the place of waters that poured into
the pool of singers. Musatta the eldress singer and Crescendjya
the younger singer are also the daughters of Aega, What mystery is this? It is of the mysteries of the galaxy. These daughters
manifest where and when needed. Not only to sing the songs of
the Bluestone Standing, but also to keep them for as long as
they stand. In some worlds these stone circles are destroyed
through the influence of the fallen. Because even they have a
right to war over the souls of the intelligent beings. They claim,
and have the right to fill their master's place of receiving souls;
the place some know as hell. This choice lays with the intelligent beings. To each, their own. Choices are made and show
who we really are, instead of whom we pretend to be. A minor
Armageddon is the dark clouds on the horizon of the blackstone
circles. The war of gods vs demons is held at bay by the hand of
the master god of the universe, known as the One Father: the
great mystery, Aine: The permeating force, the nameless, Tetra-
grammaton. Who's only earthly begotten son, the redeemer,
plays throughout all of the worlds of the galaxies with intelli-

gent life. It is he, the son, who shows his many forms and faces to all of the tribes of all worlds. Each one different according to the needs and developments of the souls gathered. Each tribe parents the souls of those found proper to their callings of life; their children.

These tribes often meet each other in the Dreamtime. Yet, they all speak the same language in the worlds of the astral, because they all speak in tongue, each one thinking they speak in their native language. The web of life is vast in time and space; it's eternal. The people of the bluestone are living in the cyclic time and can access anywhere or any time of the past, present, and future of those who live in linear time. In fact, the bluestone people access the past of the present and the present of the future. But only Tra-aega knows this. But even Tra-Aega can't access the worlds above him; the worlds of the waters that fall into the pool of the singers of stone. Tra-Aega, because he alone, has embodied the spirit of pure humility. And this is found pleasing to the lord of the universe; the creator, the cre-atrix. He who is the manifestation of all things. And to Him, all things will resolve at the end of ages.

CHAPTER TWELVE

She was perplexed, not knowing her fate. She thought she would be relieved of her station at the end of this age. Her memory of what went before was not accessible to even this most powerful seer of place and time; the center place of judgment. The soul can't be burdened with the aeons traveled. The weight of all time is too much to bear; too much to endure. We all would break down if we knew the truth of our soul's travels. One life at a time; one reality for our minds and bodies to live out. Only in the Dreamtime, and our deep meditations, can we access these worlds of wonder. We think them the creation of the mind; but creation was done, and there is nothing more to create. We think we imagine things, but in truth, it's our memories we access. We all have the universe implanted in our minds. We all travel the cyclic times without knowing. For example, if we engage in a conversation and are called away before finishing that engagement, even for a hundred years, we will return to that time and place and continue the conversation as if we never left it. We all call these memories of the imagination. Even I, as the author of this story, am simply chronicling my visions wherein all things are possible. So for me, let the sky open. Sing well, my sweet singer. Sing the bluestones that empower me to walk the blackstones of time. My arms raise and lift me to the heavens; I embrace the songs of creation. All things in the worlds of manifestation are only vibrations. Sing us real, sing us alive and dancing our life. Let those who have ears hear the soft inner voice of the singer. The songs of the Bluestone Standing.

And so it goes for Etrad-Aega. But she can embrace her fate, after all, she bore judgment on many. Some were fierce and fearsome. Such are the ways of eternity. They make their choices, and none can change that. Not even the redeemer, unless of course, he's asked to do so with deep contrition. Even the purveyor of souls has to withdraw at the gates of hell, where none are redeemed. They are already claimed by the fallen. They have relinquished their ability to see any other path. They gather focused; waiting. Waiting for the dread gates to open and receive them until the end of ages. When all things return to the center point of creation. The end of the age of ages.

The idea of beginning a new age of her judgment would be unbearable. So she worked up the elixir of forgetting. This she knew must be done. She knew from instinct, or from Tra-Aega sending her the message. Either way, she felt it was right, so she did.

Etrad again, not Etrad-Aega, because she forgot who she was once again. This is the fate of a judge who is the fulcrum of the people of bluestone. Not until the last of men perish from the earth. Whether by planetary destruction or even if they leave in spaceships or ascend to another plane of existence. She, Etrad, must stay with intelligent life to watch over them. She was here, in the beginning, she'll stay to the end.

Etrad and Tajet were left behind from the beginning of the

age. Not knowing from whence they came, or who they are. They simply followed their own instincts. This, so they didn't become consumed with themselves, and so they didn't fill their egos with false self-aggrandizement. They remained servants. They serve mankind, and mankind serves them. Without this sharing of need; there is no purpose for being. As above; so below. There can be no creator God without creation, and no creation without a creator. This is a true mystery of manifestation. The universe simply is.

Yesh, Spandrel, Tiptil, and Homa were still at the blackstone circle. Eno-Tra had no idea of where they came from. Yet he had only one day to return them to their bodies waiting in the canyon somewhere on the western continent. Spandril was still with his dead wife. She, Meandra, was unwilling to return to the land of the dead without her husband. Eno-Tra was faced with two dilemma. To force her return to the underworld, and to find the astral trail back to the canyon of bodies before they perished. Tra-Aega sent the message that he was to stay in his brother's place for the remainder of the new age. It was a shocking revelation. He felt a rebellion well up inside of him. He quashed it with pure will power. But, there lay the seed of that dread rebellion. Will it take root? It didn't in Tejet's time. He too felt the welling of rebellion when he was posted here at the beginning of the now passing age. The first time the sky opened.

Etrad did remember her sons who had no father. She remembered where they are and went in spirit to find them. A gray mist formed. Eno peered into the veil and saw a woman forming. He had no idea of who she was, or that this was his sister. Etrad stepped forth. Because she did forget her family once again, she had no idea who Eno is. "Who is this that steps into the circles of truth"? Inquired Eno. It was his own instinct that formed the question, and that question informed him of what his station was about. Because it was the first question posed to him by his brother Tajet. He had no memory of it, but it was there in his deep being. Etrad replied: "It is me, Etrad, judge of the ages of mankind". Eno knew only truth could be spoken in this circle of blackstone. But Etrad was shocked at what she pronounced. Ages? What truth is this she wondered. Did she drink of the cup of forgetting? How vague and strange a memory. She pulled herself together and added, "I am here to collect my sons, and companions of traveling. It is you who have to deliver them soon, lest they die in their bodies in the canyon of the western continent. You have to find the astral trail and lead them back home". The dark sky rumbled at these words of truth saying. An instinct welled up in Eno. A vision revealed itself, and he saw the trail. But first he had to deal with Meandra. Tajet opened the gate for her, now he must close it. That's no easy task. Where is the key? How can he do this when she refuses to go? The sky laughed. Meandra shrank in fear. Eno took advantage of this and said: "Quick Meandra, this way through the fog". Meandra didn't hesitate, and she was gone. Spandrel was angry, because he lost her goodbye hugs. Anger was not a healthy thing, even here in the blackstone circles; beasts weren't the only things that hunger. Now darkness found a path into the worlds of mankind.

Eno gathered the travelers and he gathered the mist as well. A crushing sensation engulfed the travelers once again. Eno felt it as well. This was his first time experiencing such a sensation. Confusion didn't stay long with him. He realized it was the same when Tajet brought them here. Eno followed

Etrad through the astral trail back to the canyon of waiting bodies. This time no one was enthralled with the visions of the sea. They just wanted to get home. They had the impetus of their calling bodies that were near death by now.

The surnames were dropped because of the forgetting quality of the blackstone circles. The same happened to Tajet when he was first assigned to sheriff the world of mankind. Etrad was the only one who could drink of the elixir of forgetting, yet retain some of the important memories. But only for a short time. Although she would always remember her sons. Everything starts all over again when the ages turn. But they occupy a new and higher level. New tests of will and purpose come with each new age. Until once again the sky opens.

CHAPTER THIRTEEN

Mosha sat waiting. Perplexed by the wonders he'd seen. More than that; what he felt. So deep his calling to the people, he didn't know how to proceed with a sense of purpose. His tired mind was thoroughly spent. Never before had he experienced such a drain on his abilities. He sat when he'd rather be dancing. But no, he wanted to run in circles screaming. Is this the end? The end of what? Familiarity and solid footing were escaping from his tired spirit. He heard the splashing of waters that ever dwelt at the entrance of his lodge. As if it were a far off waterfall; a strange incense pervaded his dwelling place. Ombram entered floating like a pale ghost. Lines drawn on two faces staring into each other's wetting eyes. "Mosha, what"? Mosha had no reply, just a vacancy of mind. They sat and offered incense to the empty walls. No drum could call on nothingness. No rattle could shake the spirits of not knowing. Neither man spoke beyond the question that lay flat on the floor of the shaman's hut. What? What indeed is the purpose of this strange visit from an opened sky? They shared smoke and stared into each other and went to the circles of black stone.

Eno answered their calling and invited them in. Mosha spoke saying "Who are you? Who are these people who tore open our sky"? Eno had no good answer except to relay what little he knew. He too was forgetting. The black stone circles were engulfing him, claiming him unto their own purpose. Far away across the sea, Etrad listened with rapt attention. She too was forgetting the age that was spent and done. Eno and Etrad were becoming as children freshly born, born to a new purpose; a new age. But these freshly born would develop quickly to attend their elevated stations. In the meantime, Mosha and Ombram were left without answers. They had to go and calm the people, but, for the first time, neither knew how. It didn't seem right to dance the rhythms that entrance the people, and the worlds of beast and trees. They didn't know if they faced a threat or friends. They decided to go and face the newcomers with what they hoped were words of courage. With what they hoped would bring answers. Etrad hoped for them. She wasn't yet remembering her spells and rituals; her judgements. She sat alone in her place between time and distance. Her sons, Tiptil and Homa were not with her now. They were telling tales of mystery to their people; the red-skinned ones. Enthralling them with visions of a wild sea full of nightmares. Even the bears and lions stayed in their caves sensing something was strange. This was no time for hunting. Birds stayed in their nests, and the ground crawlers were nestled in their dens. Everyone of the forest dwellers sensed a new time was fast approaching. Nothing would be the same. Their eyes and ears were wide open and they heard only the passing wind, and rivers flowing. Etrad knew. But she knew little else. She listened. She watched. She waited. What judgement was this? Judgment? What? This thought awakened her mind a little, as if a door were cracked open, and she could peer inward just a little for now.

CHAPTER FOURTEEN

There stood Tra-Aega, tall and powerful before Mosha and Ombram. The open field in which they stood was filled with people silently waiting for something. Any news from the lips of Ombram and Mosha. As if suspended in time; silently waiting. Others of the bluestone people were standing behind Tra-Aega patiently waiting to be called forth.

Tra-Aega spoke: "The stars have looked down upon you and called for newness to descend into your midst. The stars have told of a people who are ready to embrace a new destiny. We have come to fulfill their demands". He waited for his words to fill their minds. He continued: "We bring newness of life and growing onto the souls of man, you will listen to the songs of creation that will spill from what we will erect to guide you, to nourish you on your journey's throughout time. Our coming marks a new beginning for you to embrace. Do not fear the new ways and paths that we lay before you". Ombram spoke. "To what purpose is this? We have lived as we have lived for many passings of the sun, nothing has changed and we live in peace with each other, we live in peace with animals and trees". Tra-Aega answered saying: "You have lived with thoughts unrealized, with tools and machines taking form in your minds. Now is the time of realizing your purpose; your destiny. It is for you to dominate the earth and peoples to the far unknowns of this, your earth. Should the beasts grow without husbandry, you will soon be devoured and bring forth your own no more". He continued: "The stars are now in place for your favor, and we have come to build temples that will help you understand". All of the people in all of the camps fell into dreaming. These times were early and only a few camps lived on each continent. Hunting and gathering were easy things so far. Farming was unknown as it held no purpose yet. Wild were the mountains, and rivers flowed in tumultuous cascades from a high place to the oceans, and the land was heavily forested. Crossing rivers was a dangerous thing and could be done only in dry seasons. But the dwellers of rivers were hungry. Crossing rivers required the service of shamans who placated the river dwellers and the river spirits. This type of travel would hold for quite a while yet, even after the blue stone people were done. Man would labor long to build the needed conveyances that would usher in the new age. Now the fertile minds would be tilled, and the seeds of progression would be sown.

While the people dreamed Tra-Aega called forth the chief surveyor and the chief architect. He allowed Mosha and Ombram to witness the erecting of the Bluestone Standing. He allowed Etrad to witness from her place of judgment.

The architect reached out his arms and turned to the four quarters of the earth. He instantly traveled the circumference of the planet. He pulled into his mind the ley lines of power, and he marked the placements of bluestone throughout the entire earth. He gazed into the architects eyes, the architect gazed into Tra-Aega's eyes who gazed into both beings. Now, the power was set and the bluestones themselves were commanded to release their moorings from the quarries. They, the stones, broke free and floated to their place of calling. No man could lift these heavy monoliths, only the power of the bluestone gods could move them and float them into place. So they did through song. All things vibrate, and vibration is a pressure. The first song the people of the blue stone sang was a basic layer of vibrations pressure. This caused the clothing of the people to shake even as they wore them. Next, pebbles began popping up and down on the ground. Then larger stones began moving causing rock slides in the hills and mountains of the earth. The large beasts lost their footing and the wolves howled. Water bubbled as if heated and the ground melted into a liquid. Now the song intensified and huge bronze horns and bass drums were employed. Instead of the entire earth receiving the trembling, the people focused their voice onto the bluestones at the quarry. The stones they needed broke free from the quarry walls and a cushion of vibrating air lifted and floated them to their intended sites. Such was the precision of the voices. Practiced for aeons on many worlds so that no harm came to the diverse life forms. The songs had their own powers of protection. There was no cacophony, only perfect melody that in itself produced a strange harmony that melded into a pleasing sympathy as the spectacle of tons of bluestone glide effortlessly across the planes, through mountain valleys, and over the seas. The main circle of stones assembled themselves not far from the singers. Other single stones erected their massive geometries; standing monoliths at the four quarters of the earth, where the architect decided they should be. Then a flash of blue light ignited across the entire planet; invigorating the lai lines of earth. The song was done, the singers spent, and a blanket of peace fell over the planet. For the people, a bright new awakening, as if an internal sun-rise erupted from dark shadows within their minds. No more were they ignorant of who they are. No more did they see them-selves as just another form of animal. Now they understood that they were caretakers of the fauna upon which their lives de-pended.

Now, Tra-Aega called on Crescendjya. The bluestones also transcended the worlds and placed themselves in a circle on the ever-expanding planes of the bluestone world. The people who were raised up to the place of no world memories began to sing the stone songs of power. The vibrations ushered into being new worlds for new people to be born into; to be addressed, and raised up in the coming aeons. The same as had happened to the Earth so many millions of years before. When Sol was a young star.

When planets formed and settled their upheavals; the first time the sky opened. The first life was organized by the song of the bluestone people who worked in concert with the creator.

She emerged like a flashy yet pastel gemmed dragon. She arose like a flowered horse fresh from the winner's circle. Her body soft as the star petaled d'vang. D'vang pronounced simply vine. Because that is what it is. The diviners vine who's essence betrayed all false users of its purpose. A vine reaching out to all worlds, bracing and entangling itself on the blue stone circles that grew slowly across the vast galaxy. Who's presence left only a faint hint of its reality. It grew in the minds of those who un-derstand the reasons and pitfalls of living. The true believers of eternal life through redemption. Those who know they're not as holy as they'd like to think they are. To these; d'vang encircles the heart. It inspires thoughts of something more, something deeply meaningful; deeply worthy. No false admiration of who someone pretends to be. Death is the judgment of lies and pretense. Only the true heart can drink of its intoxicating esters and survive. Only the giver, never the taker. No high horse rider; no tall pedestal, no false throne of self-aggrandizement. She emerged in the blinding light of self-knowing; self-sacrifice. This is the way of the singers of Bluetone Standing. This was Musatta: this is Crescendjya. The sweet singer who vibrates the sweetest of songs; the songs of life and its evolutions.

The earth, in the shadows of ignorance, is now prepared for the bright minds who will drink its passion. The prepared and disciplined souls that gather here with ears that can sense the vibrations that are life and manifestation of all things. Crescendjya is that singer. As a child, she was allowed to play and dance in the shadows of the Bluestone Standing in circles that shed they're being for the peoples of all worlds. She understood that the bluestone was the first mineral material that formed in the beginnings of the galaxy. How she knew this remains a mystery, even to the singers themselves. Musatta watched her with close attention to her ways of dancing and playing. Musatta saw herself in this young lithe child of mystery. Crescendjya danced alone. No other child of the bluestone world played with her, no manchild took her hand to claim her for himself; she mirrored no one. And now; the song of Crescendjya.

CHAPTER FIFTEEN

Tra-Aega went into his mind's eye. He pulled hard on Crescendjya. He pulled her breath and impregnated the Bluestone Standing in a circle; in anticipation of what was to come. Etrad somehow foresaw the song and closed her ears out of instinct so that she didn't invade the sacred song with her own mind's wandering; with her own mind's ideas of what should be. She saw the people were in a trance of deep sleep and dreaming. She saw the people were lifted into empty space and set on a slab of bluestone in the void between the stars. She saw the gods gathered around them, attending them as if they were surgeons operating on exposed souls. She closed her ears but kept her eyes wide open. Then came the song.

What then is classical music, but an attempt to plagiarize the angelic choir? No man, no woman, no orchestra of the most gifted musicians could possibly sound a single vibration of heavenly perfection. Some hear it when awakening from between worlds of Dreamtime and awareness. Some; never. Crescendjya sang in this highest of quality. Every note perfectly born of the latter. She sang an aria that lasted the full dawn, and ended in the last note of dusk. The night was then silent in honor of her song as if it were a blanket of dust falling after some cataclysmic event. Crescendjya made the angels listen with heart-felt joy that silenced the harps of heaven. Even the High God on his white throne lent an ear to her musical tale of manifestation. It was He who lent His will of power to the songs and the stones of creation. It was He who guided the purpose and the results of the singer of Bluestone. It went deeply into the DNA of the people on the blue slab of heaven. The stones vibrated and echoed her magnificent tune. In perfect four thirty two pitch, transcending and humbling the clumsy brutish four forty pitch we've gotten ourselves accustomed to. Many say to our sad fate because 432 is the numerical value of creation; so this is its vibration.

The snows that fell in the north and south poles took on a perfect beautiful crystalline shape that reflected silver rays back to the source of light. All but the dark clouds of the black-stone circles bowed in silent regard. The sun shone brighter than ever before. The clouds over the oceans vaporized into pure blue sky, and then fell all over the earth as a gentle cooling showering mist that invigorated all life. The flowers bloomed no matter the season of their place. The leaves of the trees held up their green fingers to the otherwise waterless skies. Not to beg the rain that did not yet exist; but to offer praise. The Blue-stone Standing vibrated with a living heartbeat. They shook the earth fiercely, and cascades of old ice fell into the boiling seas. The people in slumber who were left on the earth dreamed the dreams of gods and glory. They dreamed the streets of gold and crystal through which all stars are made visible to the walkers of heaven. Hell slammed her wretched gates against the purity of Crescendjya's holy voice. The beasts lay down with each other, as if attending some sylvan concert never before heard.

The wolf snuggled the lamb. All was purified and made anew. The rivers stopped their manic flowing, and the whale songs of the oceans were hushed. Crescendjya sang. Tra-Aega cried his love upon the earth. Etrad fainted and dreamed her true purpose; restoring her memories. The song ended.

The people of the blue slab returned afresh, renewed and even healthier of mind, spirit, and body. Their DNA was changed and they were far less beastly than the ones left behind. Tra-Aega and his crew were done. Ombram and Mosha emerged from the shaman's hut. They too were renewed. The other camps were refreshed and awakened for the first time. Even the whales hesitated before renewing their songs.

The people no longer feared their innate talent for developing technologies. Now they understood their inheritance; their place in the world as caretakers of all life and creation. It was good; it was bad. It meant possessing things. It meant the beasts had to be tamed, domesticated and culled. These things were new.

Tra-Aega and his people left their bodies of light and returned to ship forms by which they came, by which they leave. Crescendjya slept and dreamed.

CHAPTER SIXTEEN

Tra-Aega returned to the bluestone world with his spent crew. It was the custom to dance and drink the holy and intoxicating soma in honor of the High Gods of the galaxy and the High God of the universe. They raised their voice in prayer and praise to the place of descending waters. Those waters falling now left the grasp of the erotic stones on which they long fell. They made themselves into rain droplets and sprinkled refreshment on to the people of the Bluestone Standing. It was indeed a heavenly festivity. In honor of a work well done. Crescendjya, now awoken from dreams of mystery, danced the stones in gratitude and holding the warm smile of love within her heart. The high priest mathematicians rested before working on the new time of opening sky. Before preparing another thirty years of labor for another world in need of awakening. Another song in the long history of an eternal race of beings. Musatta was beyond pleased; she was quietly ecstatic with love for her beautiful student Crescendjya. She felt so honored to be a part of this drama of Bluestone Standing. Only four or five more songs of blue stone before she could retire and hand the gauntlet of teaching to Crescendjya, and some yet unborn new student of the bluestone songs.

BOOK TWO

CHAPTER ONE

Six hundred years before Eden's strife the djinn created the akasha, the Overmind in preparation for mankind. Iblis denied the human race a thing called smokeless fire. No one knows what was denied mankind. The djinn roamed the earth with total freedom in the early times. They were the inspiration for the blackstone circles of judgment and sheriffing the world of man. This was known to the bluestone people, and it was they who were elected to control the circles. The first time the sky opened was in the beginning of creation. Tra-Aega knew them well. True they had fallen, but so powerful the magic of the djinn that Tra-Aega employed them to work the bluestone in preparation for his second coming to erect the stones and have them float to their stations on the earth according to the will of the surveyor and architect that accompanied tra-Aega. Many among the djinn were not inherently evil, they were only found in disobedience to the High God of creation. They still served mankind, but now they were caught up in the drama, and couldn't leave the earth plane. Except to go to their own place known as Jinnistan. But this place was only a close universe juxtapositioned with the earth plane of the living flesh; the children of the High God whose will was as final as was His word. It was His voice of vibration that caused the earth to exist. Men strived to abuse their power for their own satisfaction at a later time. While the heavens were in battle with Lucifer, the djinn were already here. They took up residence in the rivers and mountains. In these times the souls of the dead were also in the earth, and could wander and mix with the living. This was the vehicle through which Etrad held the power of her own spirit's wandering. They were the source of all powers known to man. Few earthlings held unity with the creator. Because of the bluestone songs, men learned many technical wonders. No more were they committed to only a few places of safety. They made stone wheels for heavy transfer which morphed into grinding wheels for grain, and wheels for chariots and wagons. The men harnessed beasts that could be domesticated to pull the plow and the wagons. At first it was a wonderful thing to be able to grow food in a single place and no longer roam the wilds to hunt and gather. But men are of a heart that embraces possessions. So some were greedy for wealth and power. They colluded with the lesser djinn and caused great upheavals and war's domination. Out of need to feed the beasts, men claimed places of their own. The djinn, being a root word for genetics, conspired to control the births of men and woman. They knew that if they caused more men than women to be born, men would raid each others camps and farms. Out of this, the djinn, among themselves drew power and station for themselves. Because their primal sin was to withhold the smokeless fire from mankind, in disobedience to the High God of creation, so they set themselves above men without the required grace of the High God of creation. So greed and illusion became their badge of calling over time. In Asia, Africa, the Americas, and

Middle East they roamed and mingled with the people. They worked to inspire wars and disrespect for women. They conspired to cause men to compete with other men for elevated honors, and diminish some of the gentler people who still held with the High God. They caused slavery, and all kinds of schemes to possess things and beings. Not out of evil, it was just their nature to heat things up and make things happen, to their own delight. Men became playthings, instead of responsibilities to be watched over. Survival was always paramount with the living flesh. Hell was on another plane, and it was empty of souls to entertain hells fallen archangel Lucifer. He was lonely, so a war broke out over the souls of mankind to populate hell, and relieve Lucifer's lonesomeness. In fact, this was the same reason the high God of creation made Adam in the first place. As above; so below, so it is said. Even Adam grew lonely and caused the creation of woman to comfort his loneliness. As above, so below meant that the earth became the middle plane of existence. The High God of creation himself set these things in motion. So as to bring strength and willpower to men who'd prefer to simply exist in comfort. But as it is with all things in the universe, force vs force keeps the wheels turning. And so it was.

CHAPTER TWO

The fallen fell into the gravity well called earth and mingled among the people. Drawn in by the beautiful women the earth produced. They had a genetic system far different from mankind's. However, they could take wives and have prodigy to enhance their existence. As was natural for their own survival on the earth. These children were demigods among the normal people. They were powerful giants who dominated the earth and its men. They built cities of great size and were heroes among men. Their cousins the Rephaim were not so heroic, they used men as slaves, or dinner if it suited them. Arrogance was their sin against the creator. He allowed them their time because men needed to grow strong. Men needed to show who they truly were in their hearts and their minds and souls. And both the heavens and hell needed a population to appease and comfort the gods, or devils, of these places. We became pawns on a multiversal chess board. The Redeemer would be called forth in his proper time. In the meantime. The battles raged. The spirits of the dead soon outnumbered the living, and now they needed elbow room. The battles raged with growing complications.

Zofas, lord of pentagrams and deep magic, came forth from his abode in Jinnistan. He sought out his people among the djinn. None would dare oppose him. He set up a city on earth from which he ruled his people. But even among them, there were rebellious ones. The battles raged. These wars brought up-heavals of continents and islands through volcanoes, floods, and earthquakes. His cities can still be found in giant ruins under the seas. He gave magical technologies to whom he chose. Some among these used the gifts of Zofas to their own purposes. And so Atlantis was born.

Out of the loins of good men, heroes too were born. Pitted against the Rephaim they grew in stature among the fearful.

CHAPTER THREE

Orlock was a true giant among the Nephilim. Standing taller than the mountain trees that grew at his home in the high cliffs. His cave was deep and with high ceilings, he rarely scraped his head on the cavern roof. His was a place where many came and drew their history of hunting and wars on the walls of the cave. Orlock wasn't feared by the local people, but invaders had a hard time with this invincible half human. His strength was only one of his virtues. His hair could be used to make strong ropes that the people used to build stone monuments as they tried to emulate the bluestone monoliths that they found on the plains of the dead. They went often to the standing stones not knowing their prime purpose. They only felt its power that provided them with the kind of health found nowhere else, not even the food could build their muscles on a level to where war was rare against them. Fast was their thinking, and faster were their reflexes. They guard this place with attentive jealousy, but they couldn't guard it against the djinn. So they called on Orlock to carve out the mountains and offer the djinn a home proper to their needs. The djinn became their ally. In time these people were ruling all other tribes. A city formed between two rivers. The battlements were as nothing before seen. Tall statues of the gods and leaders line the causeways into the city. They dreamed a dream of a tall people. Eno was one of them. He told them of the clouds of thunder and lightning threatening their existence. Because rain was unknown to them. The fields of crops and herbs were watered by the morning mist that formed everyday. It was hard to conceive of water falling from the sky. But Eno took the unruly to the blackstone circles. Of those who returned spoke of this legend. They also learned how to use the Bluestone Standing. How it was a gate to other worlds, and how to invoke gods from within the bluestone circles. These gods were people of worlds, of planets, that long held the works of the bluestone people. These brought useful species new to the earth. Horses and elephants were of great value to the people. Oxen and sheep tamed and how to make woolen clothing for the cold winters that visited when Orion was in the sky. They learned much science, mathematics and geometry that served them well. City nations emerged in time and the human dramas took on a new shape. Camps from afar came to wonder at these temples and houses built with the help of Orlock's strength. The djinn brought cedar wood, and showed them where to quarry marble, granite, limestone, copper and gold. They taught them how energy could be made to etch metal and forge invincible swords. They learned of animal husbandry, and the cutting of stems to improve their foods through hybridization. It became a place of magical wonders.

Through the aliens, they learned of the ways of kings. The alien gods built flying machines for the ruling elite. For centuries the people flourished. Because of other world wisdom and long lives of the aliens, they took the kinship into their own hands and each one ruled for centuries in their own turn.

She was at the garden pool, Mistraile loved the blue lotus that topped the gentle water. She knew it well. The court magicians were versed in its preparation and use. Through the mystical flower, she met Etrad. This is where the new city people learned of the Bluestone Standing.

Etrad received the queen well and opened up to her because Misrtaile embraced the ways of justice in the ruling of her people. Etrad had few visitors other than her two sons, and Eno who rarely came to her. Knowing no other women, she bonded well to this queen of the new cities.

"Mistraile" Ertad began, "I hope I can find proper comfort here for you, I get few visitors and I'm not really set up for entertainment" as she peered into the viewing crystal while waiting for tea water to boil on her stone hearth at the fireplace with green flames dancing. This fire was not the usual blue and yellow flame most was accustomed to. The fire wasn't really fire at all, it was of her magic; as firewood that lived in the alcove with charcoal to be seen, but not in the fireplace; just a flame burning in essence of fuel. The wood and charcoal diminished as the green flames danced, but they didn't go into the fire as a natural fire might demand; only in essence did they burn. So Etrad never had to stoke the fire, she could sleep as long as she needed to while tending the dreams so important to her station. Queen Mistraile was amused. She was used to strange magic in her temple. But Etrad's abode was something else. Stone furniture that warmed and formed to the body. Stone hugs weren't common at all. The room was pitch black, except where ever the eye fell. The floor moved in the direction she wanted to go. The queen wasn't certain of how big the room was. It was somewhere between a modest hut and a cavernous palace. Sound didn't echo as one might expect. Instead it fell into the ear like warm oil, soothing the nerves and bringing visions of the words as if they were written in the mind. In fact; speech wasn't necessary. Etrad was with a djinn, so what she wanted to communicate was more of a psychic thought transfer. This, she learned from the fire djinn. Djinn are silent, they use the mind's eye to communicate with each other. Etrad learned this when she first dreamed him. Riding a horse in the desert in her dreamtime vision, she came upon a caravan of djinn going into a pyramid that rose straight up from the desert sand. She entered by first climbing the long steps that lead to the entrance. Dark the halls and narrow the path within. Djinn walked around her, but they walked on the walls because of the narrowness in passing. She wasn't sure if it was to honor her, or to avoid her. She stepped into an empty room white as winter's birch. Empty; except on the floor lay a crocodile. A man appeared beside her. He took her hand and helped her to step on the back of the crocodile. She slipped into its scaly back, entering the beast. No fear claimed her. Inside of the crocodile was a carpet on which she sat. The carpet rose up and carried her to a high balcony she hadn't noticed before. A djinn was standing there to receive her with perfect grace, arms stretched out to invite her into a hallway that lead to an oversized throne. The one who sat on it was pure energy and glowing white. He smiled and she knew immediately she was in the presence of Iblis, lord of the djinn. Gods were no strangers to her, still, she gasped and held her heart. She almost bowed, and Iblis said: "No need to bow, I am not the high one, He is the only one you should ever bow to. Your allegiance is not mine to accept". Never before was Etrad without words. He smiled and put a thought into her head, as djinn are accustomed to do. Speaking was not in their nature, but of course, they can. Not everyone's mind was open to psychic mind transfer of ideas, An entire novel can be instantly projected into the mind; instantly understood as if an entire lifetime was written, lived, and digested. Etrad's mind lit up as if the sun rose within her. Suddenly she remembered everything she had ever lived. Iblis spoke to her softly with a deep understanding, he was a study in grace and decorum. Etrad was taken aback and wanted to match his graceful way of being. She felt so clumsy. He took pity and said to her these strange words; "Dear Etrad, The universe, my lady, is a joke upon us all, if we chose to drink of the cup that nature did not fall". He stared deeply into her eyes, she didn't understand. She receded from the throne, and found herself back in the desert. Her horse once grey was now a pearly white. She rode home and was so into her thoughts, she never noticed one step of the journey back to her cave/hut. But entering, she found queen Mistraile waiting. Etrad looked nervous because she thought she was gone too long and might've upset the queen. No, the queen was calm and composed, and they took up the interrupted conversation as if they never left it. Etrad woke up and wondered what this all meant. She gasped again, because a fiery creature was standing at her side. She stared, shaken to the core, he simply smiled and relaxed her saying; "I am a gift to you from Iblis. I will warm your abode and be the fire of your hearth. No more will you need the woodsman to deliver your firewood". He continued; "I will be the strength of your tiring years". Because Iblis revealed to her how long she's been at her station of judgment among men, now she remembered everything. She remembered her aeon with Tajet; every word spoken and every sight seen. This memory weighed heavily on her, and she fell into a deep sleep once again dreaming. A dream of ages, dark and unruly; the ages to come. The ages her full maturity would be tested by her judgement.

CHAPTER FOUR

The festive garments swirled with intoxicated bodies inside. Colorful ribbons trailing in the nights wonderful breeze that brought the perfumes of flowers from the far mountain abode of the djinn. The full moon glowed her mystery across the standing stone circle of blue monoliths. Fires everywhere one could look. People dancing, singing, drums in perfect timing and large brass horns blaring and shaking the earth all around the stones. Crescendjya's sweet refrain filled the air and awoke the stones to receive the teacher of fiery orange skin; the purveyor of souls. Angels were seen around the sky to which the standing stones pointed. This was the spring equinox and the stars were bright with promise of new life. Lithe the dancers were indeed, swinging bosom and buttocks to the singing of the breeze, the so gentle sweet breeze; further intoxicating the people. They were now in a shamanic way. They were all now receptive to the teacher, who was soon to come with angels praising the High God, in the air above, and all around the standing stones. A gray mist formed from its own center, and grew ever larger until a form appeared like a spectral shadow, between the two dolmen holding high the heavy capstone; between the trilithon portal stones. The mist held sway against the light of fires, and there stood Thoth: the purveyor of souls, the teacher, also known as Tajet in these ancient days. Tall and mighty he stood, not as Tajet-Tra, but as the god Thoth. He remembered himself after leaving the blackstone circles that took away his memories of self. Now he was in full power that he earned by sacrificing his ego for millennium, to sheriff the world of man. His face was that of a wisdom born of ages. And if the viewer looked closely with open spirit, it could be seen that his face held the shadows of an ibis, and a baboon. Thick of arm and adorned in splendor, with a writing reed in his hand. He: scribe of the gods with a voice that commanded the listener. "Let now the ways of heaven fall upon the the children of earth". All were silenced. "I am here to hold the balance between dark and light, that neither overcome the other". The people were astonished at such words, what was war for if not to overcome another? Why would darkness be of any import in the eyes of a god? More astonished were the leaders who waged wars for land, women, and life's preservation against an invader. Orlock was the most astonished. "What then am I? I, who have held armies at bay for centuries"? Thoth replied in the company of all present saying: "You are Nephilim among men, I am a god of the high God of heaven. You might rule from a mighty throne rested in the solstice of the earth, but even you will perish in time. I will rule forever, and so the equinox bows to my will alone". No one knew what he meant by these words, but Thoth speaks in the ways of mystery. Thoth had no intention of standing there forever, or of leaving soon. So he stepped from the mist and the people fell to the earth bowing. "Raise yourselves up and stand in courage. I am not to be bowed to, only the father of your souls deserve such honor. He walked with you long ago, and it was your grandfathers who forsake him. Now, only his humble envoy comes to you to bring you His word". In time will come a redeemer to lift your dead to the heavens, where you will know your destinies. Until that time, you will stay in the earth and on the earth with your blood, which is the witness of your being and your proof of being. In your blood is found the great king of all. In your heart is found the redeemer."

After hearing these words, the people wondered after him. Orlock spoke again saying: "Then, my lord: come and break bread with the people, that I might open the gates of the great palace to them, and for you, that I might invite you into our midst and counsel us in these new ways". So it was done.

The path along the land of glorious fields of barley and the pads of rice seemed to stretch out to the horizon. Waterways with arched and ornate bridges to keep dry the feet of travelers blended spectacularly with the golden sun that shined its eternal radiance across the wetlands. Hills with carved steps took the rough voyages of spirit away and gave a wonderland display of flowers and fruited trees. Then, in the path before them, stood the white marble castle with stone and wood interlaced in a dazzling display of light and color. Red and blue granite laid across the various grays of limestone and sandstone. Each vision held a fountain with marble statues of gods and heroes inviting the wanderer to seat themselves at the pools with reflective waters pure and delicious. To quench one's tongue with the pure waters that sprung up from underground rivers. Small fountains designed to wash the feet of any who would approach them. It was a scene that invited people to dance their troubles away.

The splendor of gold and silver and mercury shone all about the great hall of the people, and the king. Fine the woven cloths depicting the history of the people, beautiful tapestries hanging on the walls. Small fires and the burning of incense filled the nose and eyes. Musicians and dancers lent gaity to the festivities. A bard was called forth to sing the glory of history. These things of gaiety were found pleasing to the lord of scribes. Orlock called forth the bard to sing songs of glory honoring the battles and the heroes. To the bard Thoth said; "Bear witness to my words, my tongue is the sanctuary of truth, and my ears will know the truth, be sure of your words". Orlock wondered at the meaning of this. He knew if the self pride he harbored was revealed by the bard, he would fall out of favor with the ministers of the palace. He would fall to the true king of the people who is Betu whom he held under spells of will. Because it was Thoth who called for the bard's song, he had no choice but to let it be. So sang the singer;

> Oh, come the sons of Orlock.
> Bring your hidden daughters.
> For now at the fount of glory,
> I will spill the truth of waters.

> Bring now the warriors of blood.
> To the king and mend his brooding.
> For glory is his want.
> In war, he finds his soothing.

> Bring heros with brave tales.
> Sing of heroes blood and travails.
> Quench the fire of victory that entrails.
> Your king with wine and ales.

He sees the light in your heart.
And smells the lust within your loins.
To make strong the battlements.
That I might sing...

At this point, a dread vision of past battles, a remembrance of the true king Betu, the bard closed his eyes and wept.

Thoth rose up and placed his calming hands on the shoulders of the bard. He pulled the horrific memories of the slaughtered from the poet's delicate heart. Taking pity, he spoke into the ear of the singer of heroic wars. "Let not the piercing arrow find this heart of hearts among men". Again, the bard closed his eyes and dreamed of the healing fields of heaven.

Orlock worried only for himself at the words of the bard, and so, he was struck down by Thoth. The people were astonished. Thoth spoke to them saying "Let the silence of darkness be broken, and let it return to the silence of light, for I have said I am here to strike balance between dark and light that neither overcomes the other". Then he retired from their company.

CHAPTER FIVE

G roken the Rephaim rejoiced. His spies returned from the palace of Orlock and reported his demise. Groken's castle was massive, and filled with the spoils of his journeys to exotic places. He didn't war, he simply marched in and took whatever he wanted; especially the women. His long caravans were enough to guarantee safety in the wilds, but if anything challenged those wanderers, Groken was tall and strong enough to wrestle even the dinosaurs to ground. He stood 90 feet tall in his natural form. Towering over anything he confronted. The earth shook in warning of his coming. His muscles were stronger than the stone weaponry he rarely encountered. No one could stand against him; at least no one he met yet. Other giants were present, but far away from each other because the Rephaim didn't tolerate competition; not even their own children. If he desired a woman, he made smaller of himself to accommodate them. He was a shapeshifter with unlimited talent. He joined his seed with whatever he lusted for. His spawn were of humanlike mixed with animal attributes. Winged bulls, horse-headed men, manfish, manbird, and even trees that could walk. He needed no army. His creations were fearful enough to force obeisance from the cities of man who laid themselves down in total defeat even before he arrived. Such was the earth thunder of his passing; his signature of arriving. So he dared a march to Orlock's temple. Orlock was 110 ft tall and could stretch his arms around thickly graced tree trunks and pull them up. Groken was long jealous of him, and now would take vengeance on his followers. He desired the world for himself. The ground shook for half a day foretelling the coming of Groken and his creatures. Betu's people were now without a mighty hero. They thought to hide in the wild's, but feared the beasts as much as they feared Groken. With nowhere to hide, and with nothing to fight Groken, the priests were afraid. But they couldn't reveal their cowardness to the people. They went to Thoth for help and advice.

Enlin, the high priest asked Thoth what they should do. Thoth smiled and said nothing.

Enlin was fearful and Thoth new this.

"You could face Groken for us" Enlil petitioned.

"Yes, I could, but is this my destiny? To play protector of you who have given your allegiance to a Nephilim? Where is this power you've held over the people? Where now is your magic might"?

"Please my lord, do not abase us. We who served the people in the ways we were taught",

"Who taught you to splendor yourselves through offerings to the gods? To walk above the people in robes of golden riches. To hold yourselves above the people in arrogance and disdain"?

"We only tried to serve the spirit, and we needed to appear not as the common men".

"What god did you present to them "

"The mighty ones of the stars above us, the ones who came from the far places".

"Then go to them, I am of the stars too, but you have never called on me until now".

"We did not know of you until now".

"I have been here forever, when the first star gods arrived, before the Nephilim and the Rephaim fell from the abode of heaven where once they were above even me who has not fallen from the grace of the High God".

"Forgive us, we knew not of such things that you now speak".

"It is you who have forsaken the creator for power's sake because he abandoned you for your disobedience to Him who has tested your faith".

"What would you have of us"?

"You must return to the father and offer your contrition to Him, and to never hold another above Him. In your offerings, He is to come first, and He is to have the first born of your calves sacrificed to Him, and they must be without blemish".

So the priests went forth and made solemn their oaths to the High God of creation; they obeyed Thoth.

Thoth knew the creator would be pleased. He rose up and went to confront Groken and his evil spawn. He stood before Groken and made himself twice as tall as the Rephaim. He looked down on him, but Groken was arrogant and tried to make himself yet taller than Thoth. But the lord of wisdom diminished him instead and prevented Groken from shifting his form. In the voice of thunder he proclaimed: "You have at your disposal all of the earth with your mighty clan, but you will not touch one hair of the people of Betu. These, the mighty one has chosen unto himself because these have bowed down to the creator of man and all things under heaven". Then Thoth made small of his stature and raised his staff of power. The two peered into each other and Groken trembled for the first time in his life. He knew he could not overcome this God standing before him. He now remembered his own treason and his own falling. But he held hard his heart against the High God because he was jealous of power. Even now he made schemes against Thoth in his dark mind. His allegiance was with Lucifer, the first among the fallen. The light bringer has become the lord of darkness and kept Groken's heart in his hand.

So it was for an age of two thousand more years; until the next age comes.

Atlantis gew in power and in stature. So beautiful the island that it was the gem of the world. It was the birthplace of many sciences, magics, and philosophies. It nestled itself safe in the oceans far shore of islands and atolls. No one could threaten it. No one except Groken.

CHAPTER SIX

Wars broke out between the Rephaim. These were terrible and cost the lives of many. Groken had enemies among his own as is their want. Betu held his city away from war through the veiling of Thoth. The new city became known as Shangri la. The people of Betu built themselves temples in the high mountains away from all others. They sought the ways of husbandry and the praising of the high god. They prospered even when all others fell into dark times. The children of men became the hunted of the Rephaim. They were made slaves to go into the mines of gold and copper. The woman became their whores, and those who rebelled were slaughtered like cattle and eaten. Darker and stronger became the Rephaim. They desired to devour the whole of the earth. Dark magic has now become the weapons of war. The insults to creation did not go unnoticed. The witch women were plying their trade of enchantment and went to the beds of the Rephaim to become their bridesmaids and concubine, and to offer up their hybrid children.

"My husband" the soothsayer Limanda spoke with the sweetness of honey, "Why are you troubled"? She was the most powerful among the enchantresses. She was the chief wife of Groken, and the first among the many women of his harem of whores and young smooth bodied men and boys watched over by a strong eunuch of shiny black skin with a long spear in one hand, and a barbed flail of authority in the other.

"My dreams trouble me"

"Would you speak of them that I might soothe your fears"?

"I hold the fears of Rephaim, how would you entreat with them and live"?

"I am more than mere women, mine is a heart that beats in more than a single world, I have visited the realms of terror and failures beyond the reach of mortals".

"And you, woman, have faltered at the altar of blood sacrifice".

"Yes, but was that not my own children you devoured"?

"Those were children born of no mortal father, I know you made bed with my enemies among my own race and kept no secret of it". This seethed within him, but he kept his anger down because he needed her for her visions and her lovemaking. If not, he would devour her whole and feel her hot blood between his sharp pointed teeth. He longed to crunch her bones and this she knew well. So instead she grabbed his long thick phallus and massaged it with her soft supple talented fingers running up and down the length of his longing making it tall hot and hard as the oak wood of which his bed was made. His was a talent of its own, the serpentine nature of his erection could slither like a snake hunting the mouse. By itself, it sought out the full lushness of her swelling lips. She made deep and wide her soft haired vagina that could mold itself to her many men's needs. Or it could fold in on itself to please the moist women's place of willing lust from whoever she chose from the harem. But for now, she made ready for his self immersed plunging that bore no resemblance to the sharing of love. Only his own deep passion concerned him. He tore open many women who died screaming between his hairy legs. But she, a temptress of many, learned the ways of pleasing a Rephaim. She too was a gifted shapeshifter. And when her eyes became that of a snake, he adored her the most. By mid afternoon through hours of abusing her, he forgot his dreams. He spent his seed into her, and knowing he was preoccupied with the dream; she spell cast his seed to her own advantage. A brave thing to do that required a lot of energy to secret away from her forbidden act of treasonous scheming against him. She was avowed to another Rephaim that better fit her plans. She could not know that Etrad was watching.

A new war was to break out between the mighty Rephaim. Groken had many enemies, but only one dared to pit himself against this beast of a fallen angel.

At the camp of Shamesh, stories were told of Groken that excited the mind, and the lust of power, of this mighty one of unrivaled evil. Oh, but now the jinn were awakened to his plans because Etrad had watched the love scene of Groken and Limanda. The sorceress knew nothing of the land across the ocean that housed the effrite of Etrad who judges all things. The fire jinn laughed, and the forest trembled. Eno watched as well. Thoth readied himself for a war of minds. After all, Thoth was a trickster God, and the lord of thieves. This war, he would deeply enjoy. This war is what brought his attention to the earth when the bluestone dancers of Orlock inadvertently summoned him. Tra-Aega watched as well. He was responsible for his son's Trajet-Tra, Eno-Tra, and his daughter Etrad-Aega. It was he who would ultimately judge them all.

CHAPTER SEVEN

The cacophony of yells from the men, howls from the small beasts, roars from the larger animals, and the indescribable hissings and guttural dry gurgling trumpeting from the monstrous dinosaurs, and the trees, oh the trees, who made the air rumble with a deep sonic rubbing of their trunks and branches. Then there were the fire smiths who made weapons of metals that cannot be matched to this day. The fires deafened any who would dare to draw near to the gnomes and goblins who manned the great pits of pitch, bones, sulphur, and charcoals that were the fuel of smoking white flames that blackened the sky as far as sight would allow. Birds fell from the sky for want of a small breath of undefiled air. Hairy mastodons and oversized cousins of today's rhinos all lent vibrations that tested the spirit, and laid courage to waste. The big feet of the tusked mammals sent waves of earth-quaking messages from their deep bellies groaning to call through the miles of earth they used as a sounding board and tell each other to come and join the fray. Men, nowhere to be found, hiding in the deep caves so their frail bodies wouldn't vaporize, and hearts wouldn't burst from the violent shaking air. The ocean, twenty miles away, bubbled and caused great waves to cross the sea raising ever greater waves and molest the shores of the western continent. Even the leviathan with its prey sought refuge in the deep trenches half a dozen miles below the surface. Thoth laughed at the silly display of childish power mongering. He had seen wars between the realms of light and dark that made this earthly terror seem like a grade school theatrical play. So he watched for weaknesses that he could exploit when the drums of war called these ridiculous chest thumpers to battle.

Tiptil, Homa, and Etrad sat around the great crystal of world seeing and watched the spectacle, while the effrite djinn of Etrad's hearthfire popped corn for the audience; after all, he was there to serve her.

Tra-Aega looked concerned because he knew it was the standing stones that sponsored this development. Even he hadn't foreseen the war of heaven that brought the fallen ones, the Nephilim and the Rephaim to the drama of man's evolution through the vibrations of bluestones and the singer. He knew the High God would never allow the total destruction of the humans; lest it is by his own hand. Even then, it would not be total, He would allow the creation to continue to its conclusion even if it meant the survival of only a few and man's populations are built again. Tra-Aega worried because he feared this dread development might occur on other worlds of Bluestone Standing. He was unsure if the fallen had only fallen to the earth.

Groken had his own armies, and his sorceress Limanda to reveal the plans of Shamesh and his impossible army. Shamesh had hell to draw from; unknown to Groken. Limanda would never reveal this power hidden from Groken. She had her own plans. Let Groken be full of himself; for now. She bore his child, and too soon, that would be evident. But she didn't know hell had its own spies of the underworld.

The Rephaim called up his armies of mighty ones of his own kind, the sorceress put them under his will. These were seven meters tall, and some taller yet. All were heavily muscled and mean of temperament. Theirs was the art of accurately hurdling boulders across mountain valleys to crush each other when at war among themselves. They uprooted tall trees to use as spears and could command the winds to force each other away and bring blindness from the flying sands and larger debris. Groken was pleased with himself: he imagined he could easily overcome Shamesh, and whatever army that devil could raise. Groken had no memory of how the fall occurred, and who was the chief among them. He was naive, as all Rephaim are. But Lucifer was chief of both Nephilim and Rephaim and he loved to play the games of intelligence as much did Thoth: but not for the same reasons. Thoth preferred to trick the mind into doing the right things. Then there was the djinn of Iblis: unknown to either of the fallen ones. The djinn were experts at hiding themselves, waiting for opportunities to influence the mind; according to their own design.

Iblis called to council the house of Zofas: Lord of Pentagrams in Jinistan. As opulent as the great hall of Zofas is; the house of Iblis was that and thrice the darker beauty. His throne spread out across the wide floor its gray steps to the massive throne where he sat before the council of djinn. He called all nations of these; the most magical of all of the High God's creation. Even more so than the power of Tra-Aega, whom he also called to his dominion and presence. Seated in the great hall were the Genie, the Effrite, the Maribe, and the Jan. Four nations who dominated the magic of the four elements in the same order; air, fire, water, and earth. Lamassu and Shedu were the dread lady and lord who ruled over all under Iblis. On earth, heaven, and eventually even hell, they ruled by the magic of Nergal. The winged bull and his counterpart the winged lion.

Iblis addressed Nergal the winged bull. "Go you to the underworld of Ereshkigal and report what is disturbing the middle earth, and by whose authority this has come about. I am loath to close the book of the lion and bring such a war before the time of Armageddon". Nergal: who is also the winged lion of the open book of peace, and the closed book of war, understood only too well. And so he was willing to take on hell itself.

"I will go as the winged bull and what you say will be done, I will go to the underworld of Ereshkigal and report back to you by whose authority this war is called onto the middle earth before the time of Armageddon".

"It is good, let you go now, and take with you the five seals of passing, in order to enter the five gates that lead to the queen's throne in the underworld".

Iblis then, having called a council asked the assembly to speak what they know of this war. The first to speak was the lord of the fiery efreet

"I know of schemes within schemes, because our servant who is of the efreet among us, who has been assigned to watch over the judge of earth, who is named by Tra-Aega his daughter, she is Etrad-Aega"

"Tra-Aega has a hand in this"?

"Yes my lord, it was time for the Bluestone Standing among the children of the earth. Crescendjya sang the songs of stone nearly a millennium past, and now the fallen from the heaven have consorted with the women of men and their spawn has overpowered the children of Adam".

"This is not a good omen, the High God of heaven will not be pleased. We can not overlook this because we are already in debt to Him because we refused Adam the smokeless fire".

"And now, my lord, the sons of man are in woeful need of it".

"This cannot be, we can't allow this power among them, no matter the need. Is it not so that after this war the man-children will abuse it and bring the total destruction of all things"?

Zofas spoke up saying: "Iblis, listen to your own council, but be you aware of the far sight of the High God whom you alone disobeyed, and brought us all to this place of dishonor among the angels of heaven".

Iblis thought to rebuke Zofas, but it would not be wise to do so, because these two were equal in stature in the eyes of the High God of heaven. Iblis gave this cautious thought, he wanted no war between them in his realm. His hands were full enough as it was for now. " We make no decisions before the return of Nergal". Then he dismissed the assembly after calling forth Tra-Aega and Almeh the shaman to his throne.

No one simply waltzes his way through the gates of Ereshkigal's abode in the underworld. Not even Nergal who had not yet wrestled this queen from her throne, but he will in the far future. For now, decorum must be met. He surrendered the first of the five seals to the guardian of the earth gate. Now he had to move through the insanity that lay before him with no involvement on his part, lest he be caught there forever. This was the place of physical dominance. He saw the whips and racks of torture applying themselves to the evil children of mankind. The stripping of flesh that removed the high ego of the fallen children of Adam. The mad carnival of hysterical souls. He came to the second gate of water and surrendered another of his seals to the guardian of the gate. He entered into a vision where he was in a small craft with oars on a dark ocean, looking ahead he saw a great wave approaching him, he knew not to show fear. So he looked down as he rowed and quelled his concern. The small craft lifted up a hundred feet, cresting and down again bringing him to a shore where he disembarked and walked into a village. He saw caskets and was in the company of the walking dead. "What brings you here"? A man of black skin and remorseful heart asked him. "I seek nothing but the passing of this realm" Nergal replied. The man pointed to a coffin, but it was empty, so he let him pass through knowing it was not Nergal's time of demise. Not knowing or caring that it would never be his time. Nergal surrendered the third seal and found himself on a mountain high in the air. No way to descend, looking down he saw a mist rising up to his feet, a voice called to him saying "come my child, come and walk with me". Nergal knew there was no ground ahead of him; only empty abyss. So he stepped off of the precipice into the void. He heard a voice saying "come my child, come and walk with me' knowing there was no ground ahead of him; only empty abyss. So he stepped off of the precipice into the void. Again he heard a voice saying "come my child, come and walk with me". Again he heard, but did not listen, he simply stepped off of the precipice into the empty void and into the fire where he surrendered the fourth seal and moved above the fiery lake of screaming people begging forgiveness, but he could do nothing for them, no matter how heavy of heart he had become by now. Well he knew that they made their choices and nothing could be done for them. It was time to relinquish the fifth seal, and he wondered what new horror he would encounter? He pulled himself together and was now standing at the throne of Ereshkigal. For an instant, he remembered he had already been here, and instantly forgot. Forgetting is the way of the forces of darkness.

"Why are you standing at my throne? Did you think to interrogate me in my realm? Or do you wish to hang on my wall and wither away to nothing but flesh stretched across bone"? Nergal realized she didn't know she was talking to a lord of the djinn. He thought to seize her and take her throne. It was hard for him to remember why he came to her. She kept ranting, trying to force memory away from him. But he was the stronger of the two and this gave Ereshkigal pause; enough doubt for Nergal to regain himself and speak out. "No, you will listen to the words I speak. You will hear the words of Iblis". He had her ear now. She softened and wished to hear what news he came to bring her.

CHAPTER EIGHT

There was yet another race among men. Tall and olive skinned people of high intelligence, and of low magic. They too were as haughty as the fallen ones. They ignored the mighty ones of the fallen, and the holy ones of the high god. They too mined in labor for gold and copper, but they also knew of the power of crystals. They consorted with the lower elements of the djinn that they encountered in the deep dark mountain mines. From these, who fell from Jinistan they learned the magical science of crystals.

The olive-skinned hated the land dwellers and their constant strifes. They hated the huge beasts that made them hide themselves away. They hated working at hunting and gathering. They truly hated farming and industry. They even hated the mining that brought them into the company of the dark elves, lower gnomes, and the evil exiles of the djinn. They were lazy of body but mighty of mind. So they allied themselves with the evil djinni, and the other dark ones of the deep earth. They worked and conspired to escape the land, and create for themselves a place on the sea, where they wouldn't be bothered by the strange noisome world of mankind.

Through the dark arts they raised the seabed and carved circles of channels where they built ports and learned the ways of shipbuilding and sailing the fearsome waters that surround their keep. Concentric circles of land and channels that lead to the center where a mighty castle was built. They employed human slaves in the outer lands of the circles. They themselves made a hierarchy from lowest to royalty based on the level of science each understood. The lower the intelligence, the farther away from the center each dwelled. The outer two circles were slave keepers who tended the water ships that brought the treasured foods gathered from the sea. The fishers and long-shoremen who emptied and filled the hulls of the ships. Next inward were the craftsmen who repaired the ships. Next came the shipbuilders and naval engineers. The captains and navi-gators who did a little better in their housing and living arrangements. Then came the lesser scientists who made the technical instrument of navigation and fishing. These could ac-cess the temple of science that surrounded the main center tem-ple of magic. In this temple were the mighty crystals of unimaginable power. The lasers that sent light to wherever such powers were needed to keep the landsmen in their do-mains. From here they could control the dreams, visions, and works of the dwellers of the earth. They could burn away any threatening constructions of men and their insane fallen mas-ters. In time, they could clear the whole eastern continent of life if they chose to do so. But the landsmen had industries the islanders desired. Such as woven cloth and foods, tools and ter-racotta vessels to keep foods in. Wooden and stone tools and the gold and silver that they cherished. They developed trade, and for a time they were content. However, they were not pleased with the impending war between the fallen ones; the Nephalim and the Rephaim. The Atlanteans let the war come without interference, they were content to see what would come from the battles and decide hat might be to their their advantage when the smoke settled. What might be left for their pickings. They thought the winners, the strongest would make the best slaves.

BOOK
THREE

CHAPTER ONE

There was no plain of glory, or of honor. Only a vast desert spacious enough for the opposing camps to gather and face each other. Shamash lost the advantage of striking the city of Groken as he had originally planned. Thoth saw to that. He made sure that each had no advantage over the other. He conspired to supply spies in each city and castle. Through the mutual spies they were forced to make a truce, an agreement of battle. It was he who inspired dreams of failure if they warred in the woods or any other place. He planted seeds of doubt in the minds of Shamesh and Groken. Neither one was happy about this outcome, but both were ignorant of wars strategy on such an unheard of level. So enormous were the skills of feeding and bedding such a host of diverse creatures each with their own needs. Both had to trim the armies. Shamesh had no way of watering the walking trees in a desert. Groken had no way of supplying his giants with large rocks and uprooted trees to throw and crush the opposing horde. Thoth compelled Eno-Tra to release Meandra and bring ghosts to confound the players on both sides. She, and her ghostly band, could shape themselves into whoever they wanted. Could sew discontent by visiting the Rephaim and confounding them with lies. Then when the leaders talked to the actual men; they became conflicted. Thoth roared with laughter at the confusion. Thoth created a dream where Shamesh caught one among them making love to his personal concubine. He succeeded in causing a fist fight between Shamesh and his biggest hero of the Rephaim. Shamesh killed his own captain of his army. And to Groken, he revealed in a dream the plan of Limanda and the child seed she stole from him. The mighty seeress had to abandon him and run to the camp of Shamesh where she became his new concubine. Of course Shamesh killed his because of her perceived treason. But what good was a seeress when all was known? Except for the stolen seed, and there was no time left to claim the child was his. Now her plans were soured, and she became vengeful and unruly. Thoth roared with laughter. He was having a ball. The trickster he is went from camp to camp uprooting the plans of victory. And too, the djinn were making merry with the soldiers by causing them visions of fearful monsters, or entrancing them with peaceful visions of gaieties that brought them madness. Some were led to make love with the great beasts that swallowed them whole. In the army of Groken, the djinn caused visions of the giants to see each other as lusty women. Of course this caused uproarious laughter from both the djinn and Thoth. This was becoming a hell-spawned comedy. Both sides lost their seeress and so they they had no way of knowing what was happening to them. Thoth thought he'd die in the pains of mirth. Etrad and her sons were rolling on the floor with laughter. They spilled their popcorn.

Who wasn't laughing? Oh yes, the Atlanteans who were too arrogant and filled with their own glory to know anything of the back story. These antics even brought a smile to the face of

Tra-Aega who admired his son's playing. He was temporarily relieved. But the drama unfolding was long from ending.

CHAPTER TWO

Nergal returned from hell.

"What have you learned"?

"Lucifer has released the dead and the demons to entertain himself by attacking the men and collecting souls".

"This will cause the heavenly host to visit the earth and bring a vengeance that could well implicate us. We need to quell this battle now".

"Was it not He who made fall the Nephilim and the Rephaim"?

"It was not He who caused the dark djinn to involve themselves. He would not be pleased to find them interfering with mankind in such a way as to possibly destroy each other". Iblis turned to Tra-Aega and implicated him and Crescendjya saying "What song of bluestone brought this about? Why were the men not given the genetic ability to ward off the fallen ones"? He grew angry and continued "Now all of us are in trouble with the High God of creation, this is a mess and I expect you to clean it up. You have given Lucifer an advantage among the souls gathered on the earth".

This arose Tra-Aega's anger, he retorted "This is the work of the dark djinn that you let loose to mingle and interfere with

Nephilim and the Rephaim, why were they not contained in their abode in the mountains"?

"No, not all of this is the work of the unruly among my people".

" My son has made mirth of the war, and now it's not to be. Your sons of iniquity have taught the Atlanteans too much technology; this war is only beginning. Lucifer is now let loose among them and no good will come of it".

Nergal spoke saying "the both of you are now implicated, and the High God of creation will make judgment. Zofas must be warned of this, only he can send the pentagrams of magic to bring order among the men". This was agreed to and Zofas was once again summoned. But it was too late. The demons now caused even greater troubles.

The armies nearly destroyed themselves, and now were too thin and weak to war with each other. The demons worked evil among all of the players and caused them to quit the war and return to their cities. This might've been good, except for what they inspired.

A dark blanket of lust and licentiousness fell over the earth. Men became whores and women gave themselves to the Nephilim and Rephaim. Now were born ghastly creatures because the demons played with the genetics and caused beast and the spawn of the unholy to make love. Lion-headed men and the man-headed lions were born of the unholy alliance. Boys and girls were tortured and made the whores of the evil ones. Bear and dinosaur conjoined and brought forth beasts of proportions that threatened the whole of creation on the earth. The Nephilim and the Rephaim transformed into even taller and stronger giants who hunted all living things and made living meals of them. Forests have been ripped apart, rivers stank, and blood putrefied the land.

CHAPTER THREE

The Atlanteans were perplexed. Not liking these events, they conspired to destroy all living things. The destruction of creation would serve the demons well. They saw themselves as superior to the High God. They'd prefer Lucifer on the throne of heaven because he'd be far more exciting instead of being the patient one. He'd surely make things happen more to their liking. To rule with open dominance, and to make mankind serve them, and align the angels to their cause under Lucifer. Hell was far too confining.

They too were contaminated with the demonic forces unleashed from hell. They brought their own version of war. The leaders in the temple of magic and science conspired to create a weapon that could unleash destruction on the atomic scale. The entire building was constructed of crystal that regulated light throughout the laboratories. Long flat marble tables were laid out to work on. Many rooms with various experiments in process. Laser cutters were common, the light that empowered them were photons, harvested from sunlight and kept in a solution of liquid jade. The djinn educated them about the crystalline structures and the mathematics required to understand them. These were the djinn that rebelled against Iblis: because he sought to reunite with the High God of creation. But he still held with the intent to keep the smokeless fire away from mankind. Only Iblis held the knowledge of the strange and powerful fire that gives no smoke. So the fallen among the djinn knew only the powerful use of crystals to affect the atomic structure of creation; one step below the awful fire. Iblis is not wiser than the creator, but only the creator knows that mankind cannot achieve the evolution of becoming a spirit without the magical fire. Should men become spirit, then they would be equal to the djinn. Iblis doesn't trust men on that level, and only knows of this possibility through primal instinct, but not through knowledge. We are forever warlike and wish to dominate the galaxy; if not the entire universe. Iblis only wants to return to heaven. But of course, that's from where the universe can be gained.

The sky; being a constant blue, cloudless as always, birds and reptiles flying above, craft floating over the city. Craft using anti-gravity principles developed by the Atlanteans with the help of the djinn who bestowed technologies on the people of the oceanic circles. The warriors flew over the land and took measurements and made maps of the populated places. These advancements deluded the people into thinking they were superior and would have no troubles dominating the land bound. They were blind to the disintegrating conditions they encountered. Demons were among the Atlanteans and kept them from knowing what they saw.

The Rephaim were growing in population and in stature. Where once they were three to four meters in height, now they were approaching five and six meters tall. The mixing of genes was taking hold. They became further removed from humanity and cared nothing of lesser life forms. They were also instructed by the lower djinn who could shape-shift into taller beings and inspire evil ever darker. The Nephilim were working towards building stone monuments of power, they built gigantic pyramids that overshadowed the blue stone circles, and built their own standing stone circles from where they could journey through the galaxy. They could bring species from other planets to serve them. The Rephaim were delighted and used the stone powers to bring aliens to earth; making the demons happy. Because the first of the aliens were just as evil and brought even more advanced technology. The Atlantean craft was becoming less of a threat in the face of floating cities. Their laser beam weapons were becoming archaic. The new arrivals had nuclear technology.

CHAPTER FOUR

Tra-Aega was dismayed. He didn't foresee such events when the singers of stone enhanced the intelligence of the cosmic worlds. His intent was to be helpful, but results often disregard intent. He called counsel. Almeh, Musatta, and Crescendjya were the focus of his inquiry. Tra-Aega asked for a review of the bluestone circles erected on the plains of expansion. He knew that once erected they stood forever. He asked what could be done to shut down some of the standing circles.

"Almeh", inquired Tra-Aega: "Can we modify the stones standing? Is it possible to disempower these stones"?

"No Tra-Aega, we cannot as far as I know. This has never happened in all of the ages, and I wonder why it's happening now?"

"Crescendjya, were your songs true?"

"I believe they were Tra-Aega, they followed the traditions, singing exactly as I have learned them, and my voice never wavered from the ancient melodies"

"Is this true Musatta?"

"Crescendjya sang the songs of stone perfectly in my ear of experience. How long was the passing of time before the intelligence became contaminated with evil?"

"Only a thousand years passed before the technology disintegrated and fell into the hands of the fallen ones, they who disobeyed the High God and rebelled against his authority. But the advancement of war technologies shouldn't have come from them who prefer to do the combat in the traditional ways."

"Then, I couldn't say what went wrong, it's beyond me to know of this."

Almeh spoke: "This makes no sense, the worlds should've never known how to use the bluestone for intergalactic travels, we built many monolith, but only one circle on each planet we visited. The bluestone circles require other constructions in order to empower such journeys. What does Eno-Tra have to say about this? And Etrad-Aega? Does she offer any observations?" Almeh was most loathe to implicate Tra-Aega's family, but he had no other thoughts to offer; only truth could be spoken in the world of the ever-expanding planes of Bluestone Standing. "I suspect Iblis might be able to offer his thoughts and give an explanation, but he would have to speak from this world of truth saying, and that would be unwise and unlawful. We can't use our power to force the truth from those who would play with words. Zofas would speak with truth, but he has many secrets to protect, and so he couldn't speak openly. We have no right to put this on him, our only true choice is to go to Jinistan and hope for information that could be tested when we return. If we tried to speak his every word, we could only speak what is true, and what is false; we could not speak".

"That might be clever, but it's not the way of truth speaking because it involves trickery".

"It might be best to visit Eno-Tra and Etrad-Aega to gain information, but neither Eno or Etrad can be interrogated without revealing the truth of their origins. Withholding truth is also a lie. It might work since we wouldn't be interrogating them in this place of truth saying. I have never lied here or anywhere else in the galaxy, and I wonder at this. We can't chance their knowing, and expect them to endure an age in their stations of containment".

All were agreed; none had answers.

Almeh spoke saying: "If we council king Betu who still resides in the tall mountains away from the world of man, perhaps he could be sent to Eno-Tra and Etrad-Aega. He can be trusted with truth and has no need to know the origins of Eno-Tra and Etrad-Aega."

"Yes, that might be our best hope in these matters, but would any of those really know the true source of this evil? We will do this and see what comes next from the meetings; so be it."

The bluestone people know of hell and Lucifer, but they didn't know that those gates could be opened and release the denizens of iniquity.

CHAPTER FIVE

Shangri La, the city lost to the greater world of mankind rests in a foggy valley of the Himalayas. Now a thousand years in construction, with its own ways of drawing the gods into it. These gods were quite different from the gods that tended most of mankind. They brought the ways of meditation and were not warmongers, but of peace, yet they too could clash successfully and had their own history and technology. But the technology they gifted was not the kind that changed the DNA or mixed with the evolution of people. It was an inward science of health and mental balance. Sacred geometry was chief among the sciences. The art of communication with the intelligence of the universe through scent, color, and design was paramount in the teachings of the center planes of existence. It brought the people closer to the High God, and this was reflected in the way they lived and the fact that they lived on the highest mountains where only the strong could survive. They sacrificed the un-blemished firstborn to the High God in accordance with the ways of Able who's blood ran through their veins. Unlike the children of Cain whom they left behind because of their soft ways of self-aggrandizement and personal honor mongering. King Betu was wise in the ways of God. His people overcame the Nephilim and the Rephaim influence on their souls. They left the life of material gains before Lucifer let loose the hordes of hell on to middle earth. Before Atlantis was born and became the seat of inequity through the bastardized science spawned by the dark djinn. From their clear view of the misadventures below, and they perceived correctly the oncoming destruction of the children of Cain.

Betu, while deep in meditation and communication with the forces of his center, was told to gather the people and go into the deep caves for protection from the God of vengeance. Because he who would soon spew his wrath on the world now dominated by the Nephilim, and the Rephaim, and their human followers. In his vision, Betu was shown the cave that led to the world below the surface. Betu and his priests were disheartened to leave behind the opulent comforts of Shangri La, and the pastures they husbanded for centuries. They lived longer than any of the others, because they lived in purity and adopted the ways of good health and sharing. Primal in their lives was the obedience of the deities, and especially the high god of the heavens. Every stone raised onto the edifice of their buildings was sanctified throughout the entire process from the quarry to the cutting and shaping. They inscribed prayers on all six sides of the blocks. Some prayers were open so to be read, and some prayers were hidden on the sides that would butt themselves together as one. So now the priests had to choose between leaving them as they stood, or dismantling them and returning them to the earth. This required rituals, prayers, and deep meditation. Because everyone had to be certain they were doing the right thing. There could be no quarreling while engaged in so deeply sacred a task as is the moving of people from temples. Their minds as one, their hearts as one, and their works as one.

Colored prayer ribbons stretched high and waving in the spring air. Incense fumigating the houses and marketplaces of distribution. The temples were in fog, and the streets were misty from sunup to sunup. There were no gaps of pure air between the many scents of the different flowers, roots, and saps that were burnt each according to the person's needs and levels of understanding. What, and how a person burnt, was considered the mark of his or her position in society. Each property of the type of incense required its own science. So what a person burnt showed the level of teaching they received from the teaching priests. As a person learned more, that person moved into homes closer to the central temple. In this way, the people were motivated to be educated. The proper burning of incense was only a small part of the more important lessons of life that were taught. They learned the ways of the stone cutter's craft by first learning the properties of various stones, then the art of quarry cutting; transporting the massive blocks, masonry, cutting designs into the stone, sacred writing, and the art of depicting through sacred mathematics, and so on, all the way to priest hood which was their highest accomplishment.

The ceremonies of spring gave way to the rituals of summer. The most important summer rite was the rite of bathing. For this, a person had to meditate long hours in the melting snow. When the temperature was warm enough to melt the snow faster then the meditation could be accomplished; meant it was time to gather for the bath. The valley that led to the hot springs was five miles of trail. Everyone in the community, from child to adult, stripped naked and walked across the still cold valley to the hot springs. They spent the day in celebration and bathing. The temperature of the air was only a few degrees above freezing. The temperature of the hot spring water was a year around constant 64 degrees Fahrenheit, but to these hardy ones, that was as hot as their homes were in the winter months. The gongs rang out across the valley to inform the people that the day was spent, and it was time to return before the sunset and it would be too cold to walk naked across the valley to get back home. If they were too late, then they had to stay in the water for the night, and hope the air temperature was warm enough to return the next day. Rarely did that happen. Three times in their history did they miss the returning, and the day was disrupted so they had to work hard to make up the lost time in the fields especially. Once, a storm came while they were in the bath waters. Lightning took many souls from them. Not only did they have to carry the dead across the valley, but they had to do it before any flash floods came. While its true that there was no rain in those early times. The mountains squeezed water from the air that moved high to cross the peaks. This warm water melted some of the glaciers and caused damaging floods in the lower lands. Hunting became difficult because so many animals died in the floods. Life was wonderful; life was hard.

The mushrooms growing on the cavern walls was the vehicle of choice to travel to the Gods abode in the heavens. This was a place equal to the the place of expanding plains found in the world of the blue stone people. These were the deities of the central place of the soul. Just a notch above Jinistan, and a notch below the heaven of the High God. Here are found the two-winged cherubim. Those of God who serve mankind, wild animals, domestic animals, and birds. So the mushrooms were harvested three days before the traveling to the abode of cherubim and the deities found there.

• • • • •

Betu and his chief shaman fasted for three days while the mushrooms brewed. They meditated in silence and were left undisturbed. No Chamberlain or minister of any kind dared to approach the small cave of inner journey, where the two sat unmoving, and with eyes closed for the three days of purification before ingesting the mushrooms of traveling to such a high place of being.

Sitting together in the dark cave of visions, the two shared the journey inward to the place of purification. Lights appeared in swirling chaos; soon forming Mandela's spinning and changing shapes. These forms are in flux because they follow the time trail. When they're made of colored sands on a floor, they're destroyed immediately after the magic takes hold, usually healing or protecting. They can be used to welcome people into the temple as well. But they must be destroyed to allow the timeline to continue. The type of Mandela that Betu and his chief shaman saw were temples in of themselves, as most are. They entered the temple in their vision and were greeted by the guardians. The guardians asked them why they came and what they expected to find. This would confuse most travelers, but Betu and the shaman were accustomed to this type of guardianship. It was the same with a sphynx asking a riddle, because the asking of what they expected to find was a puzzle, seeing that no expectations were allowed in; only openness to the experience was permissible. The spirits within the temple of the Mandela decide what you need and why you came. There is no room for trickery or ego-based desires. So they said; we came only to learn. This pleased the guardians and they were given permission to enter the temple in the center. This is still

no guarantee of success. The two had to navigate the complicated path from the outermost border that can lead to the center; if they can walk the path through pure instinct. There is no map, only faith, purity, and worthiness leads a person to the center. A person has to have a serious spirit guide to accomplish this. Both men were well qualified to succeed, and this they did.

The path rose up and high around them. They now started the journey by walking the pathway that points directly to the center. Then they had to choose right or left. They extended their senses down one corridor and then the other. They both agreed the left path smelled of flowers, the right path held a small scent of decay, so they took the left path. The next choice was straight or right. They chose the right path because it pointed to the center. They chose correctly because the straight path lead to nowhere, and they'd have to retrace steps that might no longer exist, and they'd be lost forever. Now came a clearing in a topiary, they went to the center and saw that they had four choices. One path each at the four sides. Since they entered a topiary, they decided to follow the path with the high shrub borders because they knew that the path they came from would not be the same and they'd lose their determination. Of the other two, one lead through a desert and the other was dark and foreboding. So they took the path that contained life; the topiary path with the high green walls of shrubs. A crossroad appeared next. By this time they'd lost all sense of center. They were momentarily confused. They decided to sit down and see what they could perceive of the three choices. Directly ahead came a bull slowly approaching them, to the right came an eagle, and the left brought a winged lion holding an open book. Behind them an ox. Neither men had been to the Jinistan, and so they knew nothing of the significance of the four beasts. They shored up their courage and decided to follow the lion, because he held an open book, and they came here for knowledge. The lion turned and led them to two paths. One path had snakes for the whole length, the other path held rabbits for it's length. Something inside of them explained the significance of the two choices. The rabbits could bring the choice of time control, or underground hidden mysteries. The snakes could teach lessons of life and death, or the ways of transformation and growth. Now, they had to remember why they came in the first place. Death of a temple of light, and moving underground, or remaining for a time of mystery coming in the near future that might well lead to death and destruction; which in itself was a hidden mystery. Snakes and rabbits began swirling in their minds and they were becoming confused and forgetful. They both knew that when they face chaos, they should grab a thought and hold on to it until the chaos calms itself. So that's what they did. The common thought was underground, now their memories were returning and they had some hope of deciding. Betu and the shaman locked eyes and fought to quell the storm of chaos. At this point they were unsure if they chose right to follow the lion. So they became the snake, and followed its life-line to the underground dwelling of a snake hole. They saw that snakes don't dig their own holes; they borrow other animal's holes. So into rabbit they went. This time they saw many chambers and pathways, but they didn't go very deep underground. So they returned to themselves and councilled each other. Betu noted that they weren't looking to dig their way to an underground home, but that they were looking for deep caverns that were already cut by nature's waters, or magma. The shaman added that they would need the powers of transformation in order to survive underground. So they agreed with each other, and chose the path of snakes. Having made the choice and calming themselves to endure this frightening choice, the lion intervened and they saw two lions, one on each path. On the rabbit path, the lion held a closed book. On the snake path, the book he held was open. Both lions ate their books and allowed the two men to mount them. The two lions took them to the temple gates. Four gates with four beasts, one at each entrance. Now it's another choice they had to make. The gate of ox, lion, eagle, or bull. Again they counselled each other and thought of what this could mean, what did each animal signify? They decided on the art of elimination. The eagle was of the air, so they rejected it. The ox was a thing of pasture and farming, they didn't think that was appropriate. The lion was a thing of the wilds and that's not what they wanted. The bull is a thing of protection of family, so that was their choice of gates to enter the temple.

Two bulls facing each other with long horns intertwined was the lock on the tall gate of iron with massive hinges. The bulls unraveled themselves and the gate swung open.

Five steps led to the impressively decorated doors of the temple. Each step of a different color and material. The first step was a silvery metal we know as mercury, so when they stepped on it their feet sank, yet it was buoyant and held them upright if they didn't lose their balance. The next step was water and it was less bouyent, but it wasn't deep if they didn't lose their faith, although they could see sharks swimming below them. The third step was earthen and they could stand on its muddy surface only if their courage didn't fail them, or they would sink into it and be forever lost. The fourth step was truly a step of faith; it was air and opened to an endless abyss. If they were frightened and didn't mount it, then the earth would claim them. They were deeply frightened indeed, but they overcame their fear and stepped forward; they unexpectedly floated on the air. The last step was solid wood; they made the climb and now faced a great wooden double door ornate with symbols of mystery. They knocked, and it opened, making just a small crack releasing a strong scent of mushroom and blew spores into their faces. They couldn't be certain if they physically entered the brilliantly lighted chamber, or if they just stood there paralyzed and dreamed their way in; they never did know one way or the other. They did know they were on the threshold of heaven, and the council they'd soon receive would be true. Or at least as true as their inquiry was stated. Through all of the path-working of this voyage, they had no time to collect their thoughts and frame their questions.

The light blinded them for a moment as they stepped in. Lamps of the purest fire were lining the walls, the floor was an opulent yet ultra earthy green, the monuments of tall statues were lined up in two rows that seemed to stretch for miles down the center-way leading to a brilliant grayish white throne whos steps were wider than the valleys they came from. The expansive space inside made no sense considering the size of the temple from the outside. Where one would expect potted plants, there stood trees of unbelievable height and the leaves were a display of many colors splashing through the branches. A river of silver ran the length of the steps leading to the seated angel with four wings and a birdlike head. Yet he seemed more human than they were. He wore a thick garment of corrugated feathers. The piercing eyes were also soft and full of wisdom and kindness. He transformed into a more manlike appearance and spoke to them softley and firmly. From his mouth issued more than just words; it was perfect music unlike they had ever heard before. The voice penetrated their hearts and invigorated their minds. Their third eye opened and they were filled with perfect understanding. They felt time moving so swiftly it was a breeze on their flesh. A soft wind that blew away all negative thoughts. They had become so peaceful they could barely speak, yet when they did, the voices that issued from them were as angels singing God's glory. Betu and his shaman had transformed as well. They were now their higher selves and had no worries. Through the music of the angel came words of welcome. So they listened with absolute attention to the Seraphim seated before them.

"What has brought you to my domain Betu and Shref? Are you here to adore the mighty one of heaven? Or do you adore the purpose of your visit?"

Betu spoke saying: "We have come through the grace of the high God of creation. We are perplexed in our world of material, and seek an answer that is important to our people and our city."

"Yes, of this I know because I am in all places and in all times." The Angel allowed for Shref to speak also, and somehow Shref knew this.

"Holy one, upon your understanding we will destroy our city, or we will keep our city."

"You have been given words that intimidate you in your place in the high mountains. Know you not that mountains are the place of numbers?"

"I know not how to understand your words."

"You have not developed as much as you imagine of yourselves. You will grow in knowledge that will be shaped away from mankind, until the time of your emergence from the bosom of your place of pure life. You will have your own Sun in the place of no sky. You will have domesticated animals in the place of no pastures, and you will have fish to eat in the place of no rivers."

Betu and Shref looked at each other, and in that instant that their eyes fell from the angel; they returned to the cave of visions and were as if they hadn't eaten of the mushrooms. The power slipped away and left them feeling refreshed as if awakening from a deep sleep. And they understood.

The people weren't apprehensive of their return to the city in the mountains, in fact.they were perplexed and asked them why they didn't go to the cave of visions. Betu gathered his people and told them the story of the Mandela and meeting the angel with four wings. Now the people were worried that maybe the two of them had lost their senses. They said, "but you were gone only the span of milking one sheep of the herd." Sheff understood that they were gone for years because of the winds of time that kissed their flesh, and were put back in this place of time. He tried to relate his epiphany but the people insisted they were gone only for a short time. Only the ones who lived close to the temple could understand this. Sheff saw that faith was faltering and had to remedy the divide between them. He said this; "If you dream a dream that seems a long time, and you wake up in only a short time; it's as this with us." The people considered and allowed that the mushrooms in the cave of visions were at work here. But they knew the visions could last for two or three days. Some were not convinced. These conspired to stay behind in the old city and not journey to the new city. They said among themselves that living underground could not produce what Betu and Sheff claimed. They thought them foolish and would not follow. So the old city was not dismantled and they stayed behind. Sheff knew this was not a good thing, but he had to allow them their free will. Betu kept his peace; knowing there was purpos in all things under heaven. The third eye was now opened to Betu and Sheff, as it had to be in order to lead and survive deep underground.

The day was upon them, the hour had come for the leaving behind of temples and people. They spent the weeks before in preparation, taking only what their instincts told them to carry. The people held an energetic festival in honor of what they thought were the brave ones. Not knowing the fate of the leaving party, or their own destiny. The minds of these otherwise good people, whose faith was not quite strong enough, were put to sleep by the unseen angels who were always attending them. The angels wept.

CHAPTER SIX

Lucifer and his horde were gaining confidence because the High God was not destroying them. They thought that the holy one had abandoned mankind to them. They delighted more and more in the contamination of souls. They sponsored rape, murder, and all kinds of profanities against the High God's people. They were absolutely in their element. They were practicing indecencies with abandon. The dark Nephilim and the always dark Rephaim were dancing on civility as if it never existed. There was no shortage of human's willing to serve these devils. The whores were growing wealthy, and disease spread throughout the land. The demons put the men up to doing evil things to each other through challenge. They dared one man to kill the other in battles of the fist. To tear out each others tongues was a great pass time. They made bets against one or the other to do unspeakable things such as who could cut off their own leg first; the winner gets to live. The kings of men met fates evil enough to sicken even the unholy ones. Among the Nephilim their were heroes, but their numbers were diminishing because they couldn't fight against the rephaim who were growing ever taller and stronger. Some were a hundred feet tall, and maybe taller. The chests of these were shaped with perfect symmetry and they revelled in their own glory. The appetites of them grew with their expanding size, and they sought out the Nephilim to kill and satisfy their growing hunger. When the Nephilim's numbers waned, the Rephaim ate their own weaker members. Two or three Nephilim heroes towered above all others. Their heads were competing with mountains and the thin air was making their chests wider, but food was a problem. They took to grabbing monstrous dinosaurs from the seas and gobbling them whole. Wales were not safe if they happened to be within reach of these huge beings. But all life was a mere snack to them. So they ate mineral rocks, and some became ogres who were much worse. Genetics had run rampant. Birds with 80 foot wingspans mated with and lizards who were three or four hundred feet in length. The earth trembled at their passing.

Eno and Etrad were beside themselves, not knowing how to manage this. Tra-Aega was confounded and blamed himself. He fell into a deep depression and became immobile. He had no authority to destroy lives of any ilk. Iblis was outraged with his people and war was brewing between the houses of Jinistan. Even Zofas couldn't manage the evil of so many differing types. There was the dark djinn, Nephilim, Rephaim, Lucifer and his horde, ogres, Atlantis, and the growing evil of men and their whores. Children were raped and sacrificed to the hellions. Clothing made of human flesh and the bones of good men were made into spoons and knives. Competition among the evil ones became intense. Even Grocken was losing his control of the Rephaim; even though his growth was advanced and he now towered over all of the others. He still had enough loyal ones to draw up an impressive army. He wanted to dominate his domain.

The Atlanteans were hard at work with their highly advanced weaponry. The Atlanteans challenged the sea God much to their own doom. Poseidon was drawing up his own army of incredible monsters of the deep to put down Atlanta's rebellion. He couldn't do much about the land dwellers except for issuing tsunamis, and this he did. But only the tall ones would dare approach the shores, and most were out of reach to him. Deep in the ocean's depth, Poseidon pondered. He needed to protect his seas, and knew if the Atlanteans grew in power, they'd challenge him and the result would wipe out many sea creatures. He was the lawgiver in a lawless world.

The high God of creation pondered also. He wanted an end to this travesty, but he didn't want to end his creation of the earth. He made a promise to the sons of Adam that they would be redeemed. He held to his promise. He thought of sending a plague to wipe out many beings, but that would only empower Lucifer because Lucifer was the source of plagues. So He pondered knowing he had time. The promise would unfold when He sent his earthborn son: the redeemer. But that would be another age far into the future.

CHAPTER SEVEN

The people gathered 160 strong at the mouth of a gaping maw that sent strong men to their knees in fright. Betu and Enlin were forced to shore up their will and make a show of courage for the people. The mouth of the cave appeared every bit of a terrible ogre, and no one was sure if it wasn't. It showed itself at the foot of a high skull like hill with stalactites pointing down like razor-edged spearheads. Even the shrubbery seemed like a green beard. The handlike stone structure to the right of the face didn't help. It appeared that a stone giant was emerging from the ground. Even the cave bears stayed away. Sure they would be swallowed by this ogre looking monster, some people refused to enter. Now the party numbers fell. Not wanting to confront the nightmarish world that they were so sure lie beyond the descending throat. So little could be seen of the interior of the cavern; it made even the blackness a foreboding thing. A strong air current gave a sucking sound that lent to the illusion of a breathing hungry monster.

Betu and Enlin disguised a peek at each other; not at all willing to show weakness to the people. But inside each of them trembled the bones they were standing on. Betu was sure he would get sick and expose his fear. Enlin was better equipped to deal with what he saw. He, being a shaman, could use his inner sight to travel a small way into the cave. Fear kept him from going too far. What he saw was a narrowing of the passage within. Dark and foreboding as all of the others imagined. So they gathered and held council.

King Betu spoke first: "This might not be what it seems, it could well be a test of courage for any who would trespass on such sacred ground, but we were invited to enter."

Enlin added: "Hearken to your king, I give witness to what we were told."

The people weren't so sure. A spokesman called out from the crowd; "you ask us the risk our lives, and enter this dark tomb, and believe you when you claim an angel told us to do so. You say that if we don't; we'll die anyway. I see no guarantee of how we can ever return from so mysterious a place such as this. Many in the past who have entered caves never returned, why should we trust you now?" He caught himself and added; "We aren't want to dispute you in this way, but what you ask is dangerous and might well have no meaning, and we're to risk our children?"

Betu replied: "This is truth you speak. I can't fault you for showing doubt, for if it were me, I too would have questions and wonder if the visions were true. So I say to you, choose your own path and accept your own destiny. Enlin and I must obey the angel; because if we don't, and he was right, we would doom our souls rather than just our lives."

The people accepted these words, and again fell into council with each other. It was decided that those who wished to return should leave the packs behind for the ones who would journey into the cavern. They left warm clothing, a great length of rope, an abundance of food, both fresh and dry, chickens and a goat, stoneware for cooking, fire stones and charcoal with tinder sticks. Some even left heirloom poppets for protection from unruly spirits that they were certain would be encountered in the cave. So back down the grassy divide they went. The foothills seemed harsher to them on the return journey. No game showed, and the grasses were dryer than when they first left the city. They had no chief or shaman to speak of these omens. Fear engulfed them now, because either direction they traveled seemed perilous. With heavy hearts, and heavy feet, they plodded back to the city. When they came over the final rise and saw the distant city, they noticed it had lost its luster, as if a dark pall had covered it. Upon entering the gates they were confronted with an unexpected development; the city's people were engaging in evil. Loud shouts and cursing befell their ears, and the streets were littered with dead bodies. Too late, they knew they had chosen the wrong path; the path of the faithless. Finding no game and having their supplies spent, they had no way of going back to the cave. And the party that descended had a two day head start already. There was no choice but to enter the city and face their fate. They hoped their houses were still standing and secure. That hope died very quickly. Mercy had abandoned them, and their children clung to them. So it went. This was worse than the dark fate promised by the monster cave. This was real, and the further they went into the city; the darker they themselves became. They began by pushing their frightened children away. They ended with knives and swords. Their blood and their souls mingled in the dirt of the city streets.

So into the maw and down the descending throat they went, with big eyes open, to try and gather a little light from the darkness surrounding them. A firestick was struck and a torch was allowed to guide them. Since there were only 60 left in the party, three more torches were lit. They had to save resources to confront the unknown. How far the promised land? No one had a clue. Sixty men women and children navigating the dark unknown was a fearsome task. The first difficulty they encountered was a downslope in the trail, and they were able to slide on their butts and land in a chamber with stalactites and stalagmites that gave strange echoes to their voices and their breathing. They all gasped at the same time, and held their breath as one. If the ears could move forward of the body, they would've surely done so. The stench of urine and lost bowels began to overwhelm the party. They had to proceed in order to continue breathing. A bright flash of light quickly passed with a muffled bang. "Wat was that"? Six people in the back who were holding a torch blew up from the concentrated methane left behind from the others in passing. Two couples; one with two children were now lost. The people held ceremony for them as well as they possibly could. One thing they wouldn't want was spirits of the dead haunting them in a dark cavern. They were already frightened of the strange skitterings they heard all around them. Soon, as they traveled on, they heard water flowing ahead of them. The stones on which they walked were getting slippery, and worse, they were tilting down more and more. Betu and Enlin, being in front, slipped and fell down an inclining shaft that twisted left and right as if carried them to a pool deep under the earth. They panicked at first until they recovered their footing. The water was only knee deep, so they called up to to the others to follow. Yeah, sure, we'll just jump in the hole if you say so. No, they had no idea if the voice they heard was from the living or an invitation from the dead. But, angels in their kind mercy, for such people caught in a dilemma such as this, caused rocks to fall behind them. Betu and Enlin had no time to to avoid the pile of bodies that nearly drowned them. Betu went deep into the pool where he fell over an underwater ledge and was sucked down by a river current. Those who were still standing in the pool had no options but to follow him. Enlin made prayers of great power to relax the people, and give them courage to go after their king. They had to do it because of allegiance to Betu. The river current flowed rapidly and brought them to another chamber where their heads bobbed out of the water. They lost most of their supplies, and thought this to be the end. The women tried, but could not soothe the crying children. A wailing rose up and caused more rocks to fall. But this time the falling rocks exposed another chamber, unfortunately there was a shaft at the center of the chamber that went straight down. Food and many supplies were lost to the river, but they still had rope. Not sure if the rope would be enough to reach the bottom, a torch was thrown down. Whatever that torch hit gave up a loud yelp. Enlin had to go down in spirit and see what was hit before anyone else could venture down. And he had to see if the rope was even long enough to reach the bottom. As it turned out, no it wasn't long enough, and the yelp came from an animal he'd never seen before. It had no eyes, and was larger than a normal sized bull. It sensed Enlin's spirit and charged him. But of course it went right through Enlin and knocked itself out on the cavern wall. No matter, the rope wouldn't reach it anyway. The goat they brought along was long dead from panic and had run ahead without regard as to where it was going. When they found it, it was only good for eating. Chickens had given them eggs along the way, but they couldn't follow them into the river, and so they were left behind with some grain for them to eat out of respect for the spirits that watch over them. The chickens could fly and might find their way back to the outside.

Enlin found a ledge halfway down the shaft that they could reach, and it had a small entranceway to a large chamber with glowing crystals, it was their only hope. When all were assembled in the new chamber of light, it took a few moments for eyes to acclimate to the dull green of the crystals. Betu was first to fall to his knees and give praise to the angel of the Mandela. Now he knew his faith was not in vain. He saw fish all around the floor walking on their fins as if they were legs. Enlin was already busy giving thanks, and feeling deeply relieved. The dull green chamber led to brighter chambers, and some had dirt deep enough to plant the seeds they brought, and still had with them. They knew they had found their new home. The roof was high with shafts of light coming down, and some did have fruited trees and there were other chambers that seemed to go on forever. Clear clean pools of water could be found. Much exploring was to be done. Much praise was to be offered.

CHAPTER EIGHT

The technology of Atlantis had long outgrown its helpfulness for construction of docks and buildings, boats and fishing gear, flying machines and transportation devices. In fact, there was no place safe to visit anymore and that meant a dwindling trade. The routes to anywhere were claimed and watched over by the competing giants. Humans could no longer show themselves without highly weaponized guardians who treated them like cattle, which is what they'd become since they're too small to be of any real service to the giants. The fallen could no longer mate with human women because they'd outgrown them. But they were kept as baby food for the Nephilim and Rephaim spawn.

The Atlantean king looked deeply into his desire of ruling the earth. He had weapons of light that bounced off of the moon and could light a kindling stick; or an entire city. Sonic weaponry that could drive people and angels insane. Subsonic devices to cause earthquakes and landslides in the mountains to bury the ogres. Water vibrators that could bubble the ocean; he felt invincible. But what he didn't have was a way of restoring life once he destroyed it, and this vexed him. So he brought forth the scientists and commissioned them to study the foundations of life. Genetics so far was the domain of the standing blue stones and the king knew it. He'd seen the results of procreation being played out too close to the blue circles. The monstrous children of man, animal, and insect, born of the nights in revelry when the moon was hidden. These nights were not for the stones, and Tra-Aega took it for granted that dark nights wouldn't find people or animals gathered there. The land around the stones was ruffled up and large rocks and debris were to be avoided when visiting the stones. The dangers were imminent and needed the guidance of light. Every world obeyed this common sense rule. Every world except the earth, where people had become aggressively curious.

The king wanted power not only over death; but of life itself. Etrad and Eno were watching. Poseidon was looking into his assembly of water beasts who were highly psychic. Whales and dolphin-like creatures, enormous squid and other cephalopod too many to mention, but not too strange to tell of. One Kraken like monster was 600 ft long when its tentacles were stretched out, and unlike today's octopi, this one had great strength, even when reaching into the sky for an eagle to dine on. No creature was safe from the Kracken when it wished a meal. It was an interesting sight to see it hunt whales. The Kraken would silently assemble its arms deep under its victim and shoot straight up and explode out of the sea, sending waves to every shore in its path and send its prey tumbling through the sky. Then it would seem to hover while uncoiling and stretching its tentacles to their full length and gracefully land on the whale or beast, and hug the creature with its ten arms splashing through the waves. From its center it landed on the top of its query with arms gracefully splashing down with long radiating arcs across the water, and pulling the beast down to the bottom of the sea where it made its lair and dined undisturbed. Ah, but the king had more important thoughts to ponder. Atlantis was becoming an issue that needed imminent attention. Strangely, even underwater, a mist formed from within itself. A man creature took shape within the mist. Poseidon stared in disbelief. Never had he seen such a thing. He grabbed tight his trident, and stood ready to confront this uninvited brash intruder entering his domain. As the interloper became more visible Poseidon drew up his court. This is easier under the sea than it is over land where so many must travel to the assembly. The deep ocean currents brought the players to the stage. Poseidon backed himself onto his throne, and with the flush of water he drew his courtiers. Giant lobsters to act as executioner if needed. Seahorse men with spears to summon, or execute orders from the king; if needed. The throne was made of many colored coral with large opulent pearls, oyster shell inlays making the designs and sigils proper to the royal throne. The ocean is astonishingly colorful, with an unlimited array of plants and animals. He took a great delight in their colorful shells and bodies. He took them to attend and brighten his throne. The seat of Poseidon sits in the open; except for a few chalky pillars that loosely define his space. "Who is this that stands before Poseidon, king of the sea and law bringer of the lands"? Eno-Tra knew who is sitting on his throne. Eno replied: "It is I, Eno-Tra of the black stone circles who is sheriff and guardian among men of the drylands."

"What have the dry lands to do with me, Eno-Tra who is sheriff among men. Do you not know I am the lawbringer"?

"Yes, I know of you. Do you know of my sister who is the judge of the dry land people? My sister Etrad-Aega who dispenses the laws of Poseidon king of the seas"?

"No, I didn't know you, or your names. How is this to be that she who is judge dispenses my laws"?

"Yet we know of you. We have never needed to visit your domain, therefore you had no reason to know of us".

Poseidon warned Eno-Tra of his short temper and he wouldn't be spoken to in such a denigrating way. He increased his grip on the trident in his hand. Poseidon was close to unleashing his power on this imprudent visitor.

Eno-Tra pushed on, not knowing his arrogance wasn't welcomed here. "We have need of your service..."

"ENOUGH"! Cried Poseidon as he stood pointing his fork at Eno-Tra, he was on the verge of firing Eno-Tra into a watery oblivion. How dare this punk demand my service, and to a land walker yet. "You scoop up our bounty as if we're being taxed by you. As if we owe tribute to your world of parched earth." Poseidon was approaching a rage when a thunderclap shook the throne under his feet rudely sitting him back down. Even the long dark locks of his hair were showing anger, along with his wildly expressive beard. He again rose with the most threatening gesture glaring at Eno-Tra when there stood Thoth and Tra-Aega side by side with Eno-Tra. Poseidon eyed them all with growing darkness welling up from within his strong heart. Contempt and suspicion was filling him with vengeful thoughts. He, the god of laws, being disrespected in own seat of power. He'd never before seen any of this lot. He held no fear in his heart, but his mind was filled with anger. War was imminent when yet another disturbance presented itself. A chariot with horses of power and with manes that invoke the crashing of waves on the shores of destiny. In the chariot was seated Amphitrite, queen of the sea and poseidon's wife. Seated with her was Etrad-Aega. Now Poseidon understood this was a meeting of great importance. Poseidon was no one to be rushed, so after returning to a modicum of sanity, he called for a feast and wouldn't take or give words until all bellies were satisfied. No one argued at this chance to enjoy such exotic delicacies offered by the gods of the sea. The foods were not heavy and didn't weigh them down. In fact it lightened them so that each bite gave the sense of floating away like bubbles in a pool. But not in a way of confusion, just fusion. A joining of the broad expanse of ocean, It brought them to a place of calm wisdom. They each related their stories and concerns. "Amphitrite: call forth our son Triton".

CHAPTER NINE

Zofas wasn't so calm, but he was surely concerned. He was not one to travel to the earthly abode of his wayward children. He would rather leave things to them, and let them weave their own fate. He knew they played with the destiny of others, but this was over the top; had they forgotten who they are? These abandoned all reason and took to thinking themselves overlords of the earth children, and underlords of Lucifer. This he couldn't abide; especially since they sourced a share of their powers directly from him. He knew himself as one among the fallen, but he harbored hopes of redemption in the eyes of the lord. He served Iblis, but he had no choice in the matter. Iblis didn't fall in the same way as Lucifer fell. But both took innocent angels with them. Iblis was rebellious in only a single matter, and to this day he believes he did the right thing for the preservation of mankind. He doesn't sponsor man to turn away from the high God of heaven and have them follow Lucifer instead. Iblis rules Jinistan: not Lucifer's hell.

The gate of the pentagram came suddenly with no offer of the politeness or decorum that Zofas was more commonly known for. The djinn he confronted had no warning, there he was, period, with glowing eyes that said: "Here am I." The djinn of chaos suddenly lost their charm. They knew Zofas was no wayward visitor who simply stumbled into their midst. One among them slipped away. Zofas knew where he was going, and invited the result who would be Lucifer. Lucifer might hold great power over the dead and the devils with their unholy houses of demonic entities, while Zofas held power over the gates through which they came; and left. Nergal had not yet won that power from Ereshkigal, but, Zofas brought him along to judge all beings involved. Only Nergal could close the book of life, and he had the power of judgment over hell's already dead population; where Etrad-Aega could only judge the living. They knew each other from dramas long past that belong to another eaon.

The djinn who took flight from Zofas went directly to Lucifer with the tale of arival of Zofas and Nergal. Lucifer had no reason to fear the two powerful entities hisself, because he was not among the dead or the living. But he knew that Thoth would soon arrive as well. If Thoth brought Anubis, the God of the dead, then he'd have something serious to deal with. So he went to hell and petitioned Ereshkigal to unchain Azug the mad god. As much as that might add to this narration, Ereshkigal isn't a fool. If she did that, hell would be destroyed along with her, Azog, and Lucifer. Most believe the High God would erase creation if that was done. But that old goat-headed Lucifer had his own plans. The high God was watching.

The djinn love to hide, but with Zofas and Nergal demanding them to expose themselves, they had no safe harbor. Nergal stood next to the angel of Jinistan as he formed a pentagram for the two of them to peer through and see the world of the djinn in hiding. They saw the mountain caverns and rivers where the dark ones assembled and schemed. Then Zofas, with his bare hands, formed a triangle gate for he and Nergal to enter. They stepped through and were now in the world of the hidden ones. Since the djinn do not speak, no conversation was taken up. Zofas instantly saw the plans against mankind that the dark ones had initiated. He saw how the djinn gave technology to the Atlanteans claiming it was for them to escape the Nephilim and the Rephaim. How they connived to help the olive-skinned build a nation in the sea, and all the while knowing Poseidon wouldn't be pleased. They gave these people advanced crystal technology, telling them that it would separate them, and offer superiority and safety. But ofcourse they knew it would lead to arrogance and destruction. Zofas wasn't pleased. He turned his thoughts to Nergal who flashed the idea of gating the djinn back to Jinistan for Iblis to deal with. But in that case, Iblis would need some kind of holding arrangement similar to a prison, but banishment was the only punishment of Jinistan, and these dark djinns were already banished. It was known certain alloys were impenetrable by the spirit world, including the djinn. So Zofas and Nergal agreed to leave the spirit plane of these dark brothers of the djinn. They had a plan.

CHAPTER TEN

Nergal stayed on the shore, no beast of the sea would dare challenge him as he radiated fearsome energy that turned the monsters away. If they thought to attack him, their energy would leave through their feet, and be grounded leaving them weak and vulnerable. So he stood on a deadly shore in perfect safety of himself. Zofas left Nergal there and traveled through a pentagram to the innermost temple of Atlantis. The shock on the faces of the priests and scientists of Atlantis was precious, making Zofas smile inside behind his teeth. He didn't want to show arrogance to these men of arrogance. He didn't have to. The priest called up the djinn that empowered them; even before they knew what this angel wanted. They were simply outraged that such a being would invite himself into their innermost chamber of secrets. The djinn came in a swift wind of vengeance, expecting to find some intruder who'd tricked his way through the defenses erected by themselves. But when they laid eyes on Zofas, they withered at his feet. The priests and scientists wondered at this turn of events. Zofas spoke saying: "You have dishonored your nation, even though you're banished you should keep the bargains between djinn and man". This because of the refusal to give Adam the smokeless fire, they could give mankind no technologies; not even to inspire them in the minds of humans. These knew they had no defense, but they grew haughty and thought "why should we obey? Are we not already exiled"? Zofas thought back "Do you not know there are many things worse than exile?" Zofas was bluffing, but he was sure that something could be arranged, he just didn't know what at the moment. This was no time to think of such things because the djinn easily read thoughts. They can also implant thoughts, and none were better at this than Zofas. So he planted a seed, a vision of destruction and passing through the gates of hell. So strong the vision that the djinn couldn't challenge it; they accepted it, and were afraid. So too were the priests and scientists witnessing these events.

For a long time, Atlantis developed constructive technologies that helped them establish their watery kingdom. As their power grew, they turned their attention to weapons of war of incredible destruction; they had gotten carried away with the illusions of power that they now embraced. They are now in a position of dominance and thought little of using it across the earth. They too were blanketed by the dark lords of Lucifer's niche of hell. But Lucifer was also dominated by Ereshkigal and fell under her authority. She, unlike Lucifer, prefered playing by the rules. Which most often favored her, because she made the rules concerning the ways of hell. Allowing leaks of power was not found in her favor. She summoned Lucifer and told him so. But Lucifer, agreeing to follow the rules that he claimed were new to him, had one more leak up his sleeve. In the meantime, the demons were called back to hell. This may have lifted the hell-spawned blanket of darkness; but evil, by now, was well rooted in the hearts of those who adored it, and who reveled in it. It could not go on for long, this evil had to be rooted out; especially before the war against the fallen was to begin. Thoth would not allow either side to have an unfair advantage. So the demons had to be returned to hell before the final battle was to start. There was sure to be plenty of evil; even without them.

One might think the giant ones were at a dynamic advantage, but this was not so. Bodies of that size and weight could never lay down or even sit without taking great care for their knees and spine. They had to rest leaning against high rocky walls to hold their massive size. If they fell, they would be crushed by their own weight. Their ribs would collapse their lungs, and their guts would rupture from being rearranged by gravity. In the largest of them, their brains would liquify if gravity changed the structure of gray matter and blood vessels. How unfortunate for Groken; he didn't know. To him, standing sleep was natural and he had no thoughts for laying down. The ground was where the tiny ones ran about like mice; a place of filth where he dumped his bowels. He often went to the sea to cool himself. Nothing was big enough to challenge him there. Except maybe, a 600 ft Kraken.

Zofas was done with the Atlanteans with their wayward djinn. He, like Thoth, wouldn't stand for such an imbalance of power. So, he raised his hand and formed a pentagram of a banishing power, he pointed through it towards Nergal who was waiting at the shore. Nergal opened a triangle gate of passing. The djinn became smoke and made a trail that flew through the pentagram, and they manifested in front of Nergal, much to their surprise. Nergal opened the gate and the djinn were compelled to enter it. Nergal quickly closed the gate. And now the deed was done. The djinn were delivered to their own. They thought it would be easy to go about the earth and cause more chaos; but they soon discovered Zofas and Nergal had put a spell of containment on them, so they were immobile for the time being.

Zofas couldn't allow advanced technology to rest in the hands of unmonitored arrogant humans. So he councelled with Nergal and they decided to call on Thoth for his input and wisdom. They all went deep into what had happened to bring Atlantis about in the form it was. They didn't understand where the djinn had gotten this technology. A mist formed in front of them and two figures stepped out. Etrad-Aega and Eno-Tra were standing before them. Etrad spoke: "I have watched these events from the beginning, what I saw, I will relate to you. Know that I am the judge of men and not the judge of djinn. My brother standing here is Eno-Tra the sheriff of men, not the sheriff of djinn. Therefore I can't judge and Eno can't imprison the djinn at the black stone circles. But of what I know, I will relate to you". Zofas, Nergal, and Thoth listened intently because they were puzzled by the whole affair. Etrad went on; "I watched as the djinn in the mines of the mountains found time crystals which they use to travel to the future. This is breaking the laws of linear time. They paid it no mind and gathered the knowledge which one of you gave to mankind. Because of the impending war, you have no choice but to follow this path that has already been laid out before you, because the path has already been followed. Such is the way of the crystals of time. Only you, Thoth, can unwind the path, if you have such wisdom. So far, only the high God of creation has been successful in doing this playing with time. Zofas, you are so far blameless in these matters, but Iblis is implicated and that will affect all of jinistan if this isn't straightened out, Thoth is your only hope". Eno-Tra said nothing, it was for him to observe and enforce the judgement of his sister Etrad-Aega. So he would follow Thoth and enforce the decisions made by him. All of this was pointing to Thoth as the new caretaker of Atlantis. No one else could deal with matters of time as proficient as could he. So now he was known as The Atlantean. He had to make sure the weapons weren't used unfairly. After that, he would decide the direction of technology; Pandora's box was now laid wide open, and it's gifts were splayed in front of him. But, for now, Thoth had more important things to attend than Atlantis.

CHAPTER ELEVEN

Eno-Tra reflected on the events of the past thousand years he spent at the circles of blackstones. When he first came into the inheritance of the sheriff's station, his brother Tajet-Tra had no one permanently bound in any of the circles layers, now Eno had arrested many souls. Some will never return to their bodies. No one knew they had been arrested, they just continued a soulless life. Often that made little difference. These weren't people of value, they were of the ilk that would scheme up thievery and murder to get what they want. Before the fallen had arrived, there were few men or women who would transgress the laws of humanity. Now, the black stone plains had to be expanded to accommodate the crowd of newcomers. Eno was surprised at how easily a person could sell his soul in the face of even the slightest temptation. But now, with the fallen growing taller and stronger, the souls in this black purgatory were also stronger in the ways of vindictiveness and vengeance. Even if that vengeance was brought on by their own failed acts of deception. How could a person avenge himself on a victim just because the scheme backfired? He had many things to ponder. A war is brewing, and the bodies of these souls were still incarnite, and causing trouble. This troubled

Eno-Tra deeper than it should, and he knew it, but he didn't understand it.

The menacing dark cloud was growing darker, louder, and closer to the black stone circle. This caused Eno-Tra to tremble, for the first time in his life he felt a foreboding that shook his soul. It made him sick to his stomach and he couldn't control a shaking of his body. He couldn't even understand it, but it gave him a fear that was foreign to his being. He wished his father Tra-Aega were here to comfort him and explain what these things meant. The dark cloud took on a countenance of superiority over him. He had no experience to deal with this new emotion of fear and belittlement. The captured souls were suddenly cheering and looking at the dark cloud. Eno-Tra looked, and a creeping chill paralyzed his spine. In the cloud the most powerful looking man he'd ever seen was forming, The man looked familiar, but in an opposite way. He was looking at the coming of Azog Thoth, the mad God, a blind dragon who sits on the throne of chaos. Violence is what called him to enter the black cloud of the horizon. Violence and Lucifer that is. Lucifer knew he couldn't simply release the dragon chained to Ereshkigal's wall without receiving her eternal wrath. So he fed Azog a bit of news of violence each day until Azog himself was overcome with a sick desire to demonstrate his powers of chaos. Azog broke his chains by focusing on his zeal to join this war against heaven's creation. He shook the foundations of hell itself to break those impossible chains. And now he was free to smell blood and war against the high God. His goal was the destruction of mankind and the magicians that kept him sealed. Be they man or god made no difference to this dragon of flaming destruction. So now, the war was engaged, and Eno-Tra was the first to fight the chaos for which he was not well equipped because Azog would appear as a mad angel and in the next moment; a mad fire dragon. He did everything he could to invoke madness into anyone's mind. It was candy to his inner child. Tra-Aega came into the circle to aid his son. Thoth came as did Zofas and Nergal. It would take them all to defeat this monstrous dragon who was king of chaos and dark places. The breath of fire that engulfed the circle of black stone released the souls of iniquity. The roar was heard from hell to heaven and everywhere in between. Iblis shuddered at the stench of this toxic breath. He yelled out for Zofas, but Zofas was already at the front lines of this war, so he ordered the guardian djinn to secure him in his armament. He too had dragons, and with his army of dragon riders they set off for battle against the fallen. Groken has heard the battle cry and delighted in calling up his army of Rephaim and trees, he now had ogres and giants to march with him. Poseidon heard the call, and Atlantis readied their armament of terrible weapons. Their plan was to level the playing field of all comers, good and evil, to replace them with their own kingdom of technology, while Thoth was busy at war; even against them.

The trees screamed at the sight of flames bathing the entire landscape. But Grocken overwhelmed their fear of fire with the threat of feeding them to his giants, and that was a more immediate threat than even fire was to them. The trees marched into the fray against their own fears. They sunk their roots deep into the earth to suck up any water they could find at every chance they had to take a rest. Knowing that being dry kindling wasn't going in their favor at the moment. They were strong of limb and could outreach anyone. They smacked back hordes of hybridized beasts that the Nephilim brought. Giants wrestled and fell with earth quaking results, many died as soon as they hit the earth. But their crushing weight also took out many beasts and lesser giants. Humans were useless and hiding in caves and crevasses like roaches packing their bodies into cracks and hoping to go unseen. Night fell and the armies retired for the evening. Azog didn't understand this because he was blind and ruled the darkness. But as long as it was night, there was no one to war with. So he too waited for the warmth of the sun to return.

Nergal and Thoth went straight to hell and admonished Ereshkigal for what had befallen. Thoth needed no seals to pass the gates. They demanded to know how Azog came to be released. She had no answers, she didn't know the depths of deception that Lucifer would go to. The sun was threatening to rise again and they had to return to earth knowing Azug would be readying himself for more war. Ereshkigal was feeling uncomfortable with this easy coming and going in and out of her realm. She called on her spies and sent them to discover what they might. They discovered Lucifer had planted false seals at the gates of hell to let Azog out. She discovered how he fed Azog with words that enticed, and enraged him. She also discovered that she alone could do nothing about it.

Another day came and the sun rose on a scene of shining blood rivers and gore. Nephilim and Rephaim were waking to a new reality that didn't include them at the helm. Azog was the focus of both sides now, the king of chaos had no allies and didn't seem to want any. Everyone knew no one could align with him and survive, his breath alone would kill them. He delighted in his superiority. He had retreated to his throne in the black void of nowhere. So the war kept on without him for a day or two. Azog was having a good time, and he didn't want to spoil this game by winning right away. In the quiet comfort of darkness, the dragon lays in slumber and in dreams. Planning his revenge on Ereshkigal with evil plots and schemes. He knows only the dark. His are the ways of violence and only through intelligence can he be defeated and returned to the wall of Ereshkigal.

CHAPTER TWELVE

He watched and He was patient. But he was perplexed and knew something had to be done, of else the whole of creation would suffer, so he made the waters that fell from the higher planes that fell into the lapize pool of Crescendjya sparkle brightly and attract the attention of Musatta. She was ever attentive of the pool and all things that involve the singer of the bluestones. She went to the pool and looked up to see a golden cloud with many angels flying in and out of it while singing His glory. She, who sang the perfect songs of stone herself was mesmerized by the sight and sound of the high holy one's cloud of gold. A voice was sent through it saying; "I am. I am. I am". And that voice trailed off into eternity. "I am your Lord God, and I command you to obey my words". Musatta was cautious and wondered if this wasn't some kind of illusion. So she inquired; "If you are the High God of creation why do you bother with so low a creature as I am? You have never before aroused my attention, and the only thing I can do is attend the younger singer of Bluestone Standing. Of what service can I possibly be to you"? In reply, the high one took Musatta up and over the ridge from where the colorful water flowed. She gaped at the splendor of the land with streets of light; flowerbeds of luminous plants she had never before seen, castles made of gold and silver. The most beautiful women she had ever seen attended her with a love only the purest of woman could evoke, an emotion that made the old singer weep. These were the fates, the weavers, the triple Goddess. Musatta regained her senses as the three fates waited patiently. They spoke to her in soft tones of eternal wisdom that caused every cell in Musatta's body to awaken refreshed. Their message was simple; "Find a man of earth who is worthy and pure." Musatta was shocked to think that were any, given the war and evils that so plagued the earth in these days of anti-heroic plunder. She woke up at the pools edge and sprinkled her face immediately to wake up and worry. How do we find a man worthy of the high ones after we changed their inner beings by vibrating the bluestone? It was our intention to raise them up, but not to the level of holy worth. We ourselves aren't worthy of heaven's delights. Neither Musatta or Crescendjya could leave the plains of bluestone, not ever, because the stones needed constant attention; they spanned the entire galaxy. Musatta called chief Almeh and Mosha the shaman to the plain of the blue shadows, and told them what the High God and the weavers had related to her. They too were astonished and weren't sure of what to do. Tra-Aega was on the earth and at war, no one wanted to disturb him. But, the High God was watching and waiting.

The trio of Zofas, Nergal, and Tra-Aega were perplexed because of the many enemies they faced, and now this red dragon god of chaos Azog has receded into the darkness. No one knew his plans, or when or where he might emerge. And then, as if to further complicate matters, from the sky came a host of dragons with what looked like men riding them. Tra-Aega looked like he might vomit on himself when he heard Zofas laugh and even Nergal couldn't hold back a bright smile. Zofas put a hand to Tra-Aega's massive shoulder and said: "Shore up your spirit, these are the djinn with Iblis in command". Tra-Aega felt light and almost lost his footing. He was no warrior, and now he faced enemies that didn't respond to him in the ways as he was used to. No dark warrior had ever opposed him before. But these were not at all what he was accustomed to. Never before were angels and demons attacking his charges of peoples of the blue-stone that he attended diligently for aeons. Only the few souls that thought of themselves as superior to others. The evils he faced in all of the worlds of the galaxy were only nations attacking nations. Power vs power for material gains. Not a war for souls as this has become. God himself was disobeyed, and Tra-Aega couldn't condone such thoughts in the pure manhood of his shining soul. It made him sick to think of how things might be in the too real hell from where some had come to mock his cooperation with creation. With these thoughts spinning in his head, he gripped himself to greet the new arrivals from Jin-istan. Seeing dragons is one thing, but these of the djinn are much larger and far more authoritative than the normal ones a person might encounter. These, the dragons of order, and the dragons of Aine the bright one, who is the permeating force behind the universe came with wind, fire, water, earth, and the resounding voice that can vibrate everything in existence. aaahhhNNNN aaahhhNNNN came the drill, one after and on top of the other. The effect caused all to be true to themselves. This exposed spies and showed who was who without deception. Not even to oneself. Some of the Nephilim realized whose side they were really on. Some of the Rephaim quit their ways of evil and joined the ones opposing Groken. Some of the ogres realized how evil they had become and they cast themselves into the sea. Not all were affected so dramatically. Some heard it as a call to arms in favor of their own purposes. Atlantis was one of those. And the effect the chant had under the sea was amplified in the ears of Poseidon. He decided it was time to address Atlantis and their threatening ways. And Atlantis thought it was a call to action. They charged up the weapons of destruction and pointed them at the armies of Groken. Groken heard a call to action as well and decided to take Atlantis out of the picture. He led the tallest of the Rephaim and marched across the sea towards the island fortress. The waves brought on by the crossing giants destroyed the outer harbors of Atlantis and many ships were sunk even as they rested in their berths. But the king of Atlantis wasn't interested in waging a war of ships. He had weapons of light at his disposal, and he fired them straight at the oncoming Rephaim. The ones he hit were burned of flesh and lost arms and legs. The rest became outraged and as they hurried to cross the sea faster, they brought up a small tsunami that further destroyed some of the inner port of Atlantis. Tall statues fell into the sea and caused giant waves to wash over the oncoming Rephaim. The waves only pushed the armies back a small ways. In the meantime two black orbs slowly arose from the sea. As those black balls pushed upward into the sky they revealed themselves to be the bearded faces of Poseidon and his son Triton. The Rephaim never knew fear until now, facing two ocean gods who were awash with anger. A black mass exploded up and out of the water like a Nike released from a submarine. Up in force, and skyward with torrents of water falling everywhere around it. Stretching itself outward and unfolding its tentacles as if grasping the sky itself, the sun was obliterated and so were two Rephaim; hugged to death and consumed. The remaining Rephaim were left to shake in disbelief. The two that the Kraken consumed spent a few moments in a screaming mess of blood and crunching bones to entertain all who watched. Poseidon and Triton didn't hesitate to watch the macabre event unfolding. They attacked with sharp trident and conch headed spears. What was left of the Rephaim effected a hurried retreat back to the shores of safety. A spear of light arced its way through the sky and hit Triton square in his back, burning a small hole in his heavily shelled armament and gathering the amused attention of the younger god. Triton responded in like kind. He sent a spear through the miles of air and hit the weapon true to its center. The explosion was magnificent. The sky turned an ugly purple as if it were mortally wounded. Again, a wave rushed to the shore where the retreating Rephaim received it with no grace. Knocked on their butts, they became a temptation for the giant scavenger crabs, causing a mini-war between dark angel and crustacean. Hundred foot sharks were pressed on to the shore and the battle became colorful. Groken used sharks to bat away crabs, and crabs to stuff into the gaping maws of the ever hungry sharks. Groken recovered what Rephaim were salvageable and retreated back to his castle in the mountains. Poseidon and Triton turned their attention to Atlantis. So did Thoth.

An outraged god of time emerged from a gray cloud in the middle of priests and scientists congratulating themselves, thinking they alone turned back the Rephaim attack. The smoldering eyes of Thoth told them a different tale. He saw the damaged laser weapon and admonished the crew saying, "What makes you think you're successful when your weapon is smoldering from a counter-attack"? A priest answered in a haughty tone; "That was nothing, just a small taste of our abilities". As he was smiling Thoth wiped the smirk off of his rude face saying; "That was nothing is right, do you know you're up against dragons of darkness and dragons of order as well? Do you know Iblis has mounted an army of djinn to destroy you and the dark ones of his own clan, as his cold eyes found the djinn in attendance? Do you know you now face the mad god Azog whom Lucifer released from the hands of Ereshkigal? And to top things most handsomely, you've pissed off Poseidon who is marching your way even as we speak"? He continued; "Look to the raging sea, darkened with the anger of the sea gods whom you have inadvertently attacked". If the priests and scientists could shrink themselves and fall into the cracks of the floor, they surely would've. Their faces showed childish guilt that they had no way of hiding. So they began blaming among themselves. Thoth stopped them in their tracks by saying, "From this day forward, I will command Atlantis". Just as Poseidon arrived outside the gates of the high walled portion of the city. Thoth met the two titans of the sea and made a pack. "No longer will Atlantis threaten the ocean and her kind, no longer will Atlantis engage in the war against the fallen ones. Her weapons will be crushed and returned to the earth and ocean from whence they came. I will rule Atlantis from this day on until the sun no longer shines on her shore".

"Then we retreat in peace, and let peace rule over us, until the sun no longer shines on her shore". Poseidon didn't think that would be very long if he should ever have his way. The pact was done; Poseidon and Triton returned to their abode of wonder under the sea. The war over the lands beyond the shore raged on, but Poseidon had no way of waging war on dry land, so he and his son retreated from their attack on Atlantis until the sun no longer shone on her shore.

CHAPTER THIRTEEN

The Rephaim were licking their newfound wounds from the challenges of Atlantis and Poseidon. The Nephilim were wounded as well from the mad god Azog who would be showing his red wings again sometime, but no one knew when that might be. The dragon mounted djinn were ever at the ready, and thank Thoth Atlantis was calmed. Still, the war was imminent and no one was safe. The earth children were still in hiding, and the High God was threatening. This time of tense calm seemed a good time for Almeh and Mosha to deliver the High God's message to Tra-Aega. They wanted to pass it on to him through the singer Crescendjya, but that seemed cowardly, so they decided to do it themselves. But to cross to the worlds when it wasn't the right time for the sky to open was not an easy matter. It could be done, but the ceremony was long, and the preparations were even longer. Musatta stepped up to the men and soothed them saying, "Since the High God saw fit to speak to me about his desire, it should be left to me to decide how to proceed. I don't want to override your authority and I can only ask permission to make this decision". So a council with all of the people present was called for.

As night fell and the blue shadows spilled across the ever-expanding plains of bluestone; the shaman danced once again on behalf of the earthly world of mankind. The peace returned and the fires were silenced. The people fell into their accustomed spell and rose up into the void of forgetting. But this time a vision rose with them, a terrible vision of events unfolding on the earth. The people screamed some cried out loud, and some fell back to the land under them. The moons weren't in step, and fleeting chaos gripped the plains of ever-expanding bluestone. They had cracked the sky just enough for a certain red dragon to catch the scent of their world of Bluestone Standing. Azog now had a new goal, and he left the piddly war world of mankind with a greater prey in mind. A way for him to expand his plains into other worlds across the galaxy. He spread his wings and flew through the trail to the bluestone world that opened through the shaman's dance. As Crescendjya began to sing, she was knocked unconscious by what she later described as a wing of black fire that shattered and scattered across the galaxy. Tra-Aega felt the tug of Crescendjya calling. He returned to her and the blue world in spite of the war. After hearing the events of the day, he felt deep despair for the worlds of Bluestone Standing that spanned the entire galaxy.

The dragons of order on which the djinn rode spread their wings across the land and brought order, a forced order that plundered chaos and caused great harm to those of evil intent. So The Rephaim were punished severely the same as they sought to punish the innocent. They raped and ate each other, and each other's children, which only served to further evoke anger from the High God of creation. Only some of the few heroic among the nephilim went unpunished, most were torn to shreds through self warring and plundering each other; because the djinn had given them visions of deceit. The dragons demanded order, and where there was chaos, the dragons forced order making all do the right thing in spite of their own desires. They only focused on the Rephaim and the Nephilim; Atlantis was left unscathed. Thoth ruled Atlantis, but he didn't rule the scheming minds of those he left unpunished. They went to the standing stone circles and used them to call for allies from other worlds and other realms. Big success was theirs. If it were not for Azog infecting those worlds, the newcomers would've never agreed to the conditions of their calling. The still corrupt Atlanteans sought to unseat Thoth and take over from him. But Thoth is a god, not a creature of worldly creation. He himself is a trickster god, so he found the scheme amusing and didn't think it would amount to much. But over time, even a small bit of corruption can grow into a major threat. Not even Thoth realized that Azog was behind the newcomers; the aliens. He just thought they were weak minded others from distant planets. In the meantime Tra-Aega returned with the news from the High God of creation. Now they had a very real and difficult task; to find a worthy human among the hidden and fearful people who were thoroughly corrupt by the nephilim they embraced and the Rephaim they feared. Thoth, Zofas, Iblis, and Nergal were perplexed and wondered what could be done?

The gray fog with the lighter gray mist once again manifested in the company of the gods who were pondering man's fate. They watched as Etrad-Aega walked out of the mist and stood before them. She said she knows of a people who have been left unscathed by the demonic interlude on the whole earth. She included her own continent in the west as contaminated by the dark blanket of evil that fell over the entire planet, but not under it said she who sees and remembers all things.

She then reminded them of king Betu and his people in the high mountains of Shangri La. Nergal spoke saying, "Etrad, your wisdom, and your judgment are known to many worlds of manifestation, but even so, is it not so that the blanket of darkness befell the high mountains as well? How did Shangri La escape this curse of Lucifer"? Etrad replied, "My lord, even Lucifer can be tricked". This drew a proud and knowing laugh from Thoth. "Yes, it is possible that he missed a trick. Ha Ha! The trickster is tricked comes as no surprise to me". Everyone broke into tears of laughter mixed with tears of relief. "Etrad". Thoth said, "Please go on with your tale of hope". Etrad counseled them of what she knew of King Betu and his shaman Shref. She regaled them with the tales of the travels through the Mandela, its tests of courage, and the meeting of the archangel on the throne of the white palace of many splendors. How they made decisions in spite of the perplexing guardians of the path to the center. How they were welcomed and invited into the inner sanctuary where few have even so much as known about; much less sought. She went on about how Betu and Shref had to convince the people to leave the lovely Shangri La and its magical buildings and lands of splendor to take up life anew in a dark fearsome cave. A cave with an open mouth as if it were ready to swallow up the people. How some had faith and followed their king, and some whose faith faltered and they returned to Shangri La and faced their utter doom.

Nergal heard enough, he knew this cave as he knew of nearly everything underground. He turned to Zofas and said, "Yes, I can find these survivors. If there is a worthy man left alive, that's where we'd most likely find him". So it was agreed to set off for the highlands of the tall mountains and seek out these people of the deep caves. Although none were certain of the survival of the lost tribe of Shangri La. Still, it was a ray of hope to please the high god of creation, which was central to all of the hearts present. Zofas sent Nergal to find the lost tribe and bring back a worthy human.

CHAPTER FOURTEEN

Nergal is a heavy oversized winged bull, or a heavy oversized winged lion. He had no form that could pass through tight underground tunnels; even if he stood as a man he would be a giant. On the way up the mountain he called for the djinn of the mountains to obey him and act as his scouts. He knew he couldn't trust them, so he thought of ways to bind them to his will. Such ways are temporary and shaky at best. He knew he needed more than just his authority, after all, they wouldn't even obey Iblis. He flew some of the way and he walked some of the way. He was in deep thought as to how he could bind them. He saw coral spires shoving their way through the pure blue sky up ahead where the hills hid most of the city. He knew he had found Shangri La. That was no surprise for such a god as Nergal. He was, however, sickened to his soul by the sight of the city soaked in blood. Animal and human entrails strewn about, heads on pikes planted in the ground. The stench was unbearable even more so than the sights. Worms crawling on every surface, and demons on every perch high or low. Now, thought Nergal, we're getting somewhere. Nergal was no stranger to hell and it's demons. But not even he knew of the rift between Ereshkigal and Lucifer. Not to the point that each had their own sycophants. Commanding in the name of Ereshkigal gained him no traction. He was under no threat, but the demons were. Nergal went into his most stern and authoritative essence. The demons ran and hid. Nergal spoke loudly; "Run you like frightened children before me? What difference will your hiding make? I will root you out and punish you for this insolence. I will punish Lucifer if you don't obey me, and you wouldn't want Lucifer angry and vengeful because of the trouble I can cause him". They knew it was true, and little by little they emerged. The first was a brave commander of legions and confronted Nergal. "What will you have of us? Why have you come? You have no play in what we do here. Do you think our Lord Lucifer isn't appraised of our deeds? Was it not he who sent us here"?

"Yes, I'm sure his hands of evil are behind this abomination you have visited on the peoples of men. And I'm sure Ereshkigal will not be pleased to learn of your treachery".

At hearing this, the demons relaxed their spite. They knew who they're dealing with, and Nergal's words cannot be discounted or taken lightly.

"Then what is you would have of us? Are we to serve you now"?

"I will have council with your chief". And so it was, they went into a building filled with darkness and evil smells of cooking flesh; human flesh with the sulphuric scent of burning hair. Blood rivulets seeping across the floor. A table long and trenched for the draining of blood into a waiting vessel. The walls were decorated with heads of men, women and children. These heads had sight and could speak of the dread events across the globe. This was exactly what Nergal was seeking.

Disembodied voices to draw out the djinn from their hiding places in the mountains. Nergal demanded oracle from the demons. The demons were only too delighted to play this macabre game of the dead. Food and drink was offered, but only as a formality, Nergal would have none of it. Even if the food was clean he would not partake feasting with demons. So it was game time with the bodiless heads that hung on the walls. These weren't the same as they were when alive and in command of their senses. Now they're insane and untruthful; not to be trusted and put only to tricks. Nergal thought it would go better with Thoth. But when he spoke; all listened. And if any chose to disobey, then a price would be payed. That price included a one way trip to hell. The demons knew this of course, but the heads didn't share such intelligence. So now the art was to get the heads to serve Nergal's purpose, and he could expect little help from the demons. At least that's what the demons counted on. To them, this was no more than a game to be played for a price. So they pushed to set a price; an ante. The archdemon pushed forward with a plan he thought would win him an advantage. He knew Nergal had some authority in Ereshkigal's hell. But this demon's freedom to walk the earth was licensed through Lucifer. So his was the providence of intelligence. A trickster in the art of gaining unfair advantage. Nergal, knowing this, had to devise a plan that would allow the demon to gain an advantage, but not keep it. So he kept silent and unnerved the foul player of games. The demon tried to entice Nergal into a contest of wills by claiming only he could set the heads free. Nergal knew this was not exactly true. Lucifer had that power too. As did many others in the realms of hell. But they weren't here to play the game. So Nergal said, "But if I include your head on the wall, then I would have the power to set you free". The demon didn't like that. "Yes, but my head doesn't know where the king led his people, so what good would it do"? Nergal replied, "What do you think would be best, seeking a people who probably aren't even alive, or the trophy of your head"? He stroked his Lapiz blue beard as if in consideration of this thought. He saw the demon getting nervous. So he continued. "Ereshkigal makes good trade for skins to hang on her walls." Now that shook the demon because it's true. Still, he had to give in to some advantage, or the game would never end. He stared at the red eyed one in silent waiting. The others gathered around the table grumbled and were eyeing their chief with disillusion. The master of the dark party had to recover somehow. Nergal knew the ways of these demons, and knew if he walked away in total triumph, the demons would give him no peace. But what could these possibly want? He proposed this, "If you give me one head, I will not oppose your taking of this kingdom. This city will be yours until the sun no longer rises" Nergal had a pretty good idea that day was soon to come. He didn't know how, but he was sure the high god would end this travesty to creation in his good time. Surely the sun would not rise on that day. The Archdemon was growing tired of this game, and he took the only way out that included keeping his head on his shoulders. Pleased or not, the deal was struck, the game was over. The gathering of dark ones had no choice but to let it be. They couldn't bother Nergal without reneging the deal. So Nergal interviewed the heads and chose what he wanted. He asked a boy "where is your father"? The boy said "he is on the wall behind you". Another he asked, "and you? Have you family here"? The reply was affirmative. He went to an older woman and asked, "where is your husband"? She replied, "the old fool is probably dead in the big mouth cave with the rest of the idiots." So this one Nergal took. He knew the bond wasn't broken, and she'd lead him to the place her husband was, dead or alive.

What a sight to see, a winged bull with the head of a bearded man holding the head of a woman between his teeth, as if she were a lamp in the night.

It was not long crossing the valley that lead to the big mouthed cave that struck such fear in so many hearts. Nergal himself couldn't fit into the small tunnels and chambers of the cavern. He was sure their might be underwater passages to be navigated. A bull was ill-equipped for a spelunking adventure. So he released the woman and charged her to find her husband if he was still alive. She had to obey him because she was won in a game. But she thought, what a fool. I have to go and do this, but why should I return? So she did find her husband, but she was in spirit and he didn't know her. There were mountain djinn in the cave as well as the tribe of Betu. These djinn weren't so evil as to interfere with the people, as long as they kept away and didn't try to play power games with them. But there was a pact. No one could leave the cave so as to keep the numbers in balance. The only exception was human birth. But that usually held steady with human death. So the balance was kept and everyone had enough food and shelter. The people fed the djinn, and the djinn kept calamity such as caveins away. The woman had no plans to leave and return to Nergal. But he knew this would happen, so he simply followed her astral trail into the chambers of the cavern. She was mocking her husband. He couldn't see her, but the djinn could, and she couldn't see the djinn. A grey mist formed from within itself and Nergal stepped out. The djinn were amazed to see one of their chiefs emerge. They knew well who Nergal was and immediately asked about their families in Jinistan. After a friendly chat, Nergal told them of his mission. A long tale of Crescendjya's summons from the high god of creation. He spoke of the wars and Etrad's help in finding the lost tribe. He spoke of the demons at Shangri La and the massacre they caused by turning people against each other. These djinn were no part of the earth dramas, they were miners searching for rare minerals. They knew each man very well. They knew of one who was righteous to a fault. They told Nergal how this man could be trusted as long as he knew it was about obeying the high god of creation. Of how he spent his free time in meditation adoring the creator. Of the work he did for both man and djinn. He was a good carpenter, and a good husband. Nergal was pleased. He told the djinn he would take this man with him to meet the High God. The djinn told him that could only happen if a trade for another human was done. Nergal said, "didn't you see I brought one"? She never knew of the deal because she couldn't see the djinn. She only knew her hopes of escape were dashed, and she strangely felt compelled to help her husband. She came to him as a lover in dreams, and gave him advice. As it turned out, she once again became his wife.

CHAPTER FIFTEEN

Everyone was licking their wounds in retreat of the wars. And now new players arrived thanks to the Atlanteans who discovered the traveling powers of the blue stone monuments. Now were aliens from worlds and realms. Flying ships were common, new technologies piled on the old. New alliances between the star men and the others of earth who tried to dominate the planet. They especially came to the western continent to make bases undisturbed, and to contaminate the red nations with wonders that they used more for domination than for teaching or advancing. But the people learned by watching and by serving. So, even in the world of the great plains and tall timbers with rivers that carved out the land, there were flying machines and monumental architecture. Pyramids sprung up all over the planet. These to communicate and guide others to the pearly planet with wispy skies. The star people could move tons of stone as easily as did Tra-Aega and his team from the bluestone world. They knew the methods of joining stones to create electrical fields by which they powered their machines. They smelted ores, built forges, and used metals to create tools to put the humans to work gathering more ores. Gold and Aluminum were their most important metals that they used for commerce across the galaxy. Mineral gems such as ruby, garnet, diamond and many others were of great value in intergalactic trade. The star men also knew much about genetic manipulation. They brought forth an array of new species transformed from the common to work as they needed. Foods for the many different kinds of aliens required a lot of differing genetic design. Hoisting slabs and digging out mountains required heavily muscled beast that also had specialised food variations. Humans were genetically manipulated to endure deep mining in hot environments. They were intellectually advanced, but only to a certain point. Smart enough to serve, dumb enough not to revolt. In these ancient times life spans were long. Most people lived for centuries. The star men could live for thousands of years. Some did and ruled for their entire lifetimes. This overlaps the events of the blue stone drama. Atlantis wasn't the first to utilise the stone monuments in this way. Betu was one of the star men who lived for a thousand years. Many people in this story lived for centuries. But now Azog was in the mix. The newcomers had no thought for the traditions they were upstaging. They were filled with evil intent and came to dominate and enslave. This was not lost on Etrad or the gods of the bluestone and the djinn. It was just another complication in the mix with the fallen. It seemed that many forces gathered to exploit the pearly planet with the wispy skies.

Nergal returned with his nomination for the god who would seek a worthy human. This human was also in servitude. He was a servant of the creator God. Humans had not yet gained independence or self will. In fact, no one asked him his name. Was he Utnapishtim? Noah? It depends on who tells the tale. Leave it to be that he served, and served well. He had a knack for carpentry, and understanding of natural engineering. Tell him your idea, and he produced the form. He brought dreams to reality, and that is why the djinn favored him. If were any other than Iblis, Zofas, or Nergal who had asked for his release from the caverns of the deep earth; he would still be there serving the people and the djinn. Some say it was the High God of creation that affected his release. None is left to say with any certainty. Either way, here he is and now what?

Nergal wondered at this situation where he journeyed forth in behest of the High God, and now what was to happen? Etrad didn't know, not even Tra-Aega from whom the request was issued. Tra-Aega inquired from Crescendjya and Musatta and came up blank. No one knew what to do with the holy man. To make matters worse, the holy man had disappeared, and no one could find him; not even Etrad. Now, what indeed?

The war didn't disappear. Once again the drums were heard as Groken reared up again to mount another assault on the Nephilim. Atlantis was no longer a threat to him, and he had allies among the djinn who promised they would stand against the mounted dragons of Jinistan. There's were the dragons of chaos. Fierce and powerful dragons that challenged everything of order. Azog was out of the picture because he was busy on other more advanced planets of greater interest to him. But because he was awol from Ereshkigal's wall of flesh, she was now in the mix. She had access only to earth because that's where the fallen had fallen. However, she did have the power to bring him back to hell because that's where the high god of creation installed him with the help of Thoth and other ancient gods and goddesses such as Sekhmet; the lioness- headed goddess. That war was incredibly bloody and required Sekhmet to walk volcanic fire across the planet. She could be quenched only by a lake of beer. Ereshkigal didn't want to invoke her; she was too hard to control if she had to rise up to the level of fighting the mad god Azog. Sekhmet prefered the peace that came with her great fiery power. She sits on a fiery volcano that is her throne.

So now there is war once again. Dragons vs dragons are a terrible sight. What happens when ultimate power meets ultimate power? Blood! Storms and rain clouds were unknown so far on the earth. A mist enveloped the planet in those early days, a mist to bring precious water to the living plants and trees. But now the vision of sky had changed and brought fearsome sights of dark clouds of thunder and lightning. No rain, unless you call blood rain, then you might say it stormed. Dragons are unkind to each other when they're at war. Cats can be cruel, but dragons mean to rip flesh in a show of power and domination. Some breathe fire and some breath toxic fumes or even ice. They dive from the high sky at supersonic speeds and grab each other with clawed wings that can make some of the weaker ones explode in midair. Sending acid rain to the ground where nothing can survive the stinking assault. Breathing is impossible during these battles, so anyone who wishes to survive needs to be tucked far away from the sky battle. That means, on the other side of the mountains. Many humans were carried across mountains to safeguard them. The Nephilim did this to preserve their slaves. Zofas was on his dragon and commanding the forces of the djinn. Nergal had his own wings and was many times more fierce than any dragon. Imagine a flying winged bull of immense size battering flesh of any kind. The dragon didn't simply explode, it vaporized; rider and all.

The Nephilim returned from the mountain hideaways of the humans. It was for them to tackle the Rephaim and make war against the trees. The sky was filled with battle and the severed body parts were falling all around. This clash of titans was heard in heaven. The High God of creation looked down and saw the man He called Upnashtishtim. He sent Uriel to him to deliver a message. "Build an ark, a boat of these dimensions". The man looked at the plans and cried out. "What would you have of me? I am a man and can't possibly move such timbre, I can't even cut such trees as this craft would require". The angel told him, "It is the Lord of Heaven that commands you. Surely you have enough faith to believe in him. He will not let you labor alone".

"To what purpose is this craft to be so huge and mighty? Am I to carry it to the sea"? Uriel smiled saying: "No, the sea will rise up and come to you when you finish. When you have loaded two of every animal, one male and one female of each animal that comes to you." The man of godly worth thought he had lost his mind at last. He already doubted his sanity just from being removed from the cave where he had spent his entire life. Shocked to the core by what he had experienced when unbelievably flying in the air on the back of a winged bull which scared him to near death, and now this? I have lost my mind was the recurring theme that ran through his thoughts. He had no idea what to make of the war in the sky with body parts falling all around. He thought this must be the result of a volcano he heard tales of when he lived safely underground. Or it was just his madness. Uriel took pity on him and placed his hand on the man's shoulder and instilled peace into him. Uriel told him that his brothers would be brought to him to help build the ark. In the meantime, he should go about the land and speak to those humans who might listen and be saved from destruction. He told him that it's plain to see that with so much evil in this world, there had to be cleansing to preserve mankind. Visions were given to Utnapishtim so he could see the evil at play all about him, and this would give impetus to his preachings. And so, once again, he obeyed.

CHAPTER SIXTEEN

E trad came and told Nergal what had befallen Utnapishtim who will be known as Noah also, she said. "He has been given many names so he can be remembered everywhere in the world. There will come a day when mankind will speak in different tongues because although evil will be washed from this planet, men will still have evil in their hearts. They will have free will and that will bring struggles born of competition. But in this way, the High God of creation will know his men and chose among them who will be his followers." Nergal was a deep thinker and wondered what they might be chosen for? He related the tale to the others in his camp of djinn, and the blue-stone god of circles, as he referred to him. The war raged on, the demon inspired technologies were growing stronger and it became obvious that the real goal was to challenge heaven itself; the fallen wanted it back but in their own hands this time. Meanwhile, the worthy one preached and Nergal had the task of retrieving Utnapishtim's brothers from the cave of the djinn. This time he came prepared and brought the priests of Atlantis to offer in trade. Angry and fearful as the priest might be, they could not know that Nergal was saving their lives. Because this cave world would survive the oncoming waters of renewal. Evil had to continue its playings with mankind, or else the redeemer wouldn't be needed, and men could never claim an abode in the kingdom of the High God of creation.

It was time for Tra-Aega, Eno-Tra, and Ertad-Aega to withdraw from the earthly realm and return to the blue stone world from where they came. Soon, many of the standing monuments would be destroyed and their work was done. Mankind had evolved into a willful species of their own. Many lessons were learned, and many technologies as well. Thoth would reincarnate as he always does after the flood destroys Atlanta. He had tasks to finish first and could afford to ignore the remaining throws of the battles of the fallen. With the blending of genetics between the peoples of man, the fallen, the aliens, and beasts; there was surely enough good and evil to make for future choosings of the evolving souls. Evil, as a ruling entity was done. Now it would become just contamination no different than a virus; a flue. War would still be dominant; but not the eating of nations. People would no longer be seen as slaughtered cattle for the dining table. Where human flesh was eaten; disease would reign. Cannibals would still be among mankind's children, but it would be rare and costly to any who would partake. All things in their own time and this applied to the newly won free will of mankind. But still, now, the battle raged.

CHAPTER SEVENTEEN

The camps of the dragons were a vision not to be missed. When they slumbered, it appeared that the ground was rolling up and down with their breathing. Some exhaled fire even when sleeping. Some exhaled toxic fumes, and some breathed with thunder from their throats. Tails of different colors and shapes poked up and down like masts of ships. The tips of those tails were of various geometries; some spades, clover-like, straight and pointed, straight and forked. It was a garden of strange delights. Dragons can change their sex at will. Although sex wasn't the focus when at war. So many sleeping dragons, it seemed like the earth herself breathed.

Morning came and the sun did rise, so did the hordes of war. The battle came early because Groken wanted to surprise everybody. Every dead body was his hope, but he, a fallen angel, was facing gods and angels that hadn't fallen so far. He was left with his trees and dragons, but the Rephaim and ogres took heavy losses. So the surprise attack didn't go so well for him. Nergal was back from the cave people and he was refreshed and ready for a fight. Thoth was still in Atlantis, but that could change quick as mercury. The aliens were now the biggest threat. They had technology that dwarfed the old Atlantis lasers and sonic weapons. The aliens had nuclear weapons, and they weren't bashful about using them. In fact they took out an area where the Atlanteans were in the process of building a pyramid for their powers of communication with other aliens. The sky now has waring dragons and waring flying ships with devastating weapons that showed no mercy on their targets. The black cloud that once hovered at the far reaches of the black-stone circle was closing in on it. Thunder and lightning were its calling card, but now rain could be seen falling from it for the first time ever. Thirty years had passed since the acquisition of Utnapishtim, and he had warned everyone about this day for decades; no one listened. He even warned the fallen, but they had no ear for this comedy of a ship that couldn't fly, and couldn't float because it was so far from the deep waters of the sea. But Nergal was more sympathetic and went once again to the cave of the djinn. He collected people to be saved, even with no one to trade them for. He was a high lord of the djinn and they had to obey him. So he took brothers and sisters of Utnapishtim to the ark that was in the process of loading animals; two of each kind. Their were a lot of animals in those days of genetic mutation. Many of the beasts refused to board the strange building thinking it was some kind of slaughterhouse. So even the animals rebelled against the will of the High God of creation. Nephilim laughed and Rephaim tried to crush the ark. But the ark was protected with a holy shield that even the aliens couldn't harm with nuclear bombs. Those bombs were all duds and not one would explode. One would think the aliens might take this as a sign of power beyond them, but they held hard hearts and harder heads, they refused to admit anyone was beyond them. Azog was called, but he couldn't return because Ereshkigal had him entranced. He was now willing to return to hell. The sky grew darker. So dark and strangely threatening that the sky ships and dragons retreated from their battles. They waited in their safe cavern harbors to watch the sky and see what would happen.

Utnapishtim knew what was coming, he had to make preparations for the animals. He had to make sure enough food was on board. He didn't have to feed any beasts, because they weren't in their bodies, they were in genetic form. But when he revived them, they would need food and life support of many kinds. He and his relatives worked diligently with Thoth at Atlantis' labs to create this science of survival. In the meantime the Nephilim gathered humans to their large cities to protect them. They were kept busy building statues of the Nephilim and Nergal whose likeness adorned every wall and entrance to every temple. Nergal was much adored for the services to man and angel that he performed. Many monuments came into being using the many new technologies that the earth acquired through djinn and alien. The Rephaim were easier to control now that their numbers were diminished. The cities prospered under the heroic Nephilim. But still, the less heroic, and the ogres were at their games of evil shenanigans. They were hungry and the cities seemed like a good hunting ground for easy prey. Especially now that Iblis, Zofas, and Nergal took the dragons of order back to Jinistan because they saw what was coming from the angry hand of the High God of creation. Tra-Aega returned to the bluestone world with Eno-Tra and Etrad-Aega. Ony Thoth was left behind with the humans and the warmongers. Only Thoth had the power to rise up and avoid the storm that was sure to come. The aliens had a chance to escape, but they were too full of themselves and mocked the ark and the storm. They had storms on their worlds, so they weren't afraid of a little rainfall.

Thoth was busy with his work of turning the Atlantean technologies into something useful. He knew the high god was going to reduce the population because of the types of evil that had befallen mankind. He knew that some would survive, and the ark was probably mankind's only hope. So he worked at mapping out the human body and working the ways of medicine and health. He was knowledgeable of the human body, and that mankind had an amazing amount of energy flows in the body. So he made many medicines and books of knowledge that would help the people in the same ways that the people were helping the animals to survive. He could not abandon mankind to save himself. So he prepared ways to reincarnate himself. For this, he went to the heavens and consulted with archangels and the high god himself. "You will have these powers and this knowledge" is all the high god said. Then Thoth returned to the earth and went to the desolate places to meditate on these things. A dragon as large as the sky appeared to him, it said its name is Pymander and it represented the High God of creation. The dragon gave Thoth technology over crystals that was new to the earth knowledge. Thoth could now cause the atomic structure to resist oxidation and last forever unscathed by any threat of fire, breakage, or the oxidation of time. He wrote of the technology of Atlantis, but he hid those writings away in order that they're preserved for mankind in some distant eaon. He foresaw that in the next age to come, he would write on other crystals what mankind would need to preserve the spirit of life. How many of these eternal books had he written? As many as there are ages of life. Each age will reveal its own book of knowledge according to its needs. For now; the flood.

CHAPTER EIGHTEEN

Drums resounded, horns were blown, and a great noise rose up from the ark. The animals were secured and now the gangway would be withdrawn and the door sealed shut. But Utnapishtim first gave all creatures, including man and the fallen ones, a chance to repent and enter the ark. The Nephilim didn't think they needed such protection because of their power being so ultimate. The Rephaim mocked the ark because of their innate arrogance. And the men and woman went along with the fallen because they viewed them as so powerful, and the ark builder was viewed as a fool. So they conspired against the ark and danced around it singing foolish songs. Worse was the kindling they placed around and under the ark. They set fire to the kindling and the giants fed whole trees to the flames. Now they danced with total abandoned, It would've made the demons proud if they were still on the earth instead of safe in hell's all-embracing flames.

The fires blackened the sky so much that the dark clouds that now hung over the earth was invisible to the dancers. The people across the sea on the western continents ran to the high mountain caverns and hid themselves away. Only a few were successful. Etrad-Aega was no longer there to protect and guide them. In the high mountains, where the eagles made a feast of them, and the long snakes embraced them and ate well. The tall bird people of the Nephilim danced a strange hoop dance that foretold of their return. These birdmen were not friendly and they ate many people, but they also recognized the importance of the tribes and found honorable the man tribes adoption and preservation of the sacred. So they made a pact with the people that when they returned from the land of the dead they would no longer eat them. Instead, they would teach and protect them. The birdmen knew that mankind was destined to evolve beyond the primitive state they were in for now. They also foresaw the destruction of the fallen because of the low state humanity had slipped into. There was no ark on the western continent. The people sealed themselves away in the deep caves and discovered a world of advanced beings deep under the earth. They joined with those, and learned many things. They kept the ways of sacred paths and knowledge.

Outside of the ark, a great noise arose. People, aliens, Nephilim, Rephaim, ogres, and even the trees screamed and yelled for Utnapishtim to open the door to the ark. But the ark was sealed and the voices went unheard; unanswered. The rain burst forth from the sky and the groundwater swelled up. The seas raised thousands of feet. Poseidon was confounded because the sea wouldn't obey him now. He had to watch with a heavy heart while the ocean ate the land. While the seas joined with the fallen sky waters. And the ark lifted up from its moorings. There was no rejoicing inside of the ark. Only horror at the thoughts of what lies outside; what had befallen the people of little faith.

It is said that the rains fell for forty days and forty nights. No one really knew because the sun was obliterated from the sky. There was no way to tell time. The rain and the rising seas conspired to bury mountains and offer no dry land as a refuge. And so the promise of 'until the sun shines no more' was kept. All had died accept the fish. When the earth drenching storms finally subsided, the ark stilled its bouncing and jerking about. The rogue waves no longer assaulted the frame, and the people were no longer seasick. Utnapishtim opened the one small window and the rush of fresh air reinvigorated the crew. He awakened the genetics of the small birds first, bringing them out of the cryogenic state he had kept them in. He released them one at a time until one dove returned with greenery in its mouth. Now, it was known that the flood was receding.

The people of the western continent stayed underground for a long time after the flood. It's known from their legends that they emerged from caves thousands of years after the flood. By this time humans were well established on the eastern continents. Great societies had come and gone by then. The Nephilim had returned, but not in the fallen state of old, now they were helpful and less corrupt. They had learned their lessons well. So many monumental structures came into being. All over the earth, they had their influence.

BOOK FOUR

CHAPTER ONE

The private jet landing at Oakland International Airport carried only one passenger who was holding a package that looked like it might've done fine in the mail if it were boxed properly. But instead, he held close the package, and his was an expression of tired relief that the plane was indeed landing. Professor Chang looked like a man who could've used a few more nights of sleep. He was no drinker and not under the influence of any drugs; legal or not. Security looked at him with a wary eye. But then they looked away immediately and forgot what they saw. He slipped through the checkpoint with no questions asked. The package he hugged so dearly had an iridescent glow that should've brought notice to him. But the professor knew it wouldn't gather so much as a blink. He made it through the busy airport to the waiting limo with a huge sigh of relief. It wasn't the guards that he worried about, it was something else that he would rather not remember he ever saw. Now, he wasn't sure he could convince anyone of what it was that took interest in the package. So far, he only gained an invitation to the archeology and paleontology department of Berkley based on his reputation. He'd published many of the textbooks used at the University.

"Professor Chang"? The chauffeur inquired as the man walked up to him.

"Yes, it is I, and please waste no time delivering me to Professor Mornet". He hesitated and asked if the professor was at the college lab.

"My instructions are to bring you to the private residence"

"Oh dear, that's not what I expected, I asked for a secure meeting".

"Yes, I understand, I am Professor Mornet's concierge, and I am to assure you have the most strict security".

"Very well then, but we must move along the most public of roads". Chang said as he slipped into the limo seat that was directly behind the driver but on the passenger side. He wanted to be able to observe everything.

The concierge would give no argument, it was his to follow instructions in the most accommodating way possible. "Yes, of course, as you require. But I must instruct you that the last half mile is a private road through a wooded topography".

"Oh dear, well there is no time to hire a helicopter. We'll take our chances having no alternatives" He said this as a test of confidentiality.

"Yes, professor Mornet has informed me to take the most secure of measures. Please relax sir, the ride will take a bit less than an hour". The driver replied in a way that showed himself competent.

Professor Chang took that in good faith, knowing that this man was indeed close to professor Mornet. He had to be highly trusted. "That will do", as he loosened his bowtie. "I must nap for a moment". As he hugged the package even closer. The driver noticed Chang tried to conceal the package by covering it with his jacket. And so he allowed himself a hidden smile.

The limo turned onto a beautiful section of tree lined road-way offering shade from the bright sky above. A fierce looking dark cloud off to the left threatened a storm that the concierge took notice of. He took a deep breath and continued on the path.

"Professor Chang"? The driver spoke softly, "we have ar-rived, and I shall repair you to your rooms if you'd like". Chang was about to protest and demand an immediate audience, but a quick glance in the mirror told him its best to freshen up a bit first.

The rooms, indeed, spoke of wealth and elegance. Chang had only seen such opulence when he visited a chalet in France, when he was a student of a tall prominent archeologist who took him under his wing. He wondered at the wisdom of con-tacting this one first. But it was too late to reconsider. He made the best of things, knowing that few could understand the sig-nificance of his iridescent package.

"Professor Chang, how pleasant to meet you here, I trust the trip was refreshing". The woman was amazingly beautiful as if a princess from a fairytale.

"Yes, of course, all arrangements were superior". He hesi-tated. She noticed, and replied, "You seem astonished that I'm a woman, but I assure you I am professor Mornet". Her brilliant smile couldn't be argued with. "Please allow me to invite you into my study and we shall discuss this strange relic of yours". She then called forth her concierge for a whispered exchange. "He shall bring refreshments as we speak, I would be most grateful to share your adventurous tale of this finding". Chang thought that a strange thing to say. He looked around and took in the sights of the high tech world he'd have to become accustomed to during his stay in America. He expected curt profes-sionalism from Professor Mornet, and not a sharing of his ad-ventures. After a long chat, he opened the package and a blue light spilled out with an incredibly pleasing vibration. He no-ticed how she looked at it with a strange fondness. He thought to inquire of her reaction just when the concierge returned with a well-aged wine that professor Chang was hard pressed to name. He was no wine connoisseur, but he was a distinguished man of the old world and should be able to recognize so fine a vintage. The wine put him in a dreamy state of relaxation. So he returned to his tale of finding the relic outside of normal archeological digs in the sands of the Iranian desert. Not too far from Petro, the ancient city of the djinn. As he went on, the stone relic began glowing brighter and he could swear he heard a heavenly voice singing. He experienced a vague feeling, as though the truth of his words were somehow being judged. As he drifted into a deep comforting sleep, a grey mist grew over the relic.

The concierge looked at professor Mornet and said. "Etrad: is it that time again"?

"Yes Tajet" she sighed "I believe it is".

EPILOGUE

Once again the genetics of the High God of creation is being challenged and played with. Once again the earth is threatened by the runaway results of high technology and genetic manipulation. Still, mankind has no smokeless fire to moderate the need for technological evolution that could ultimately dominate and destroy all life. With the smokeless fire, mankind could evolve into a spirit being of light instead of a nuclear fueled quantum society bent on domination of the galaxy.

We, of so fragile a vessel as our bodies provide, would imagine ourselves above all of creation. The truth seems that we are interdependent of all things good and evil. Salt is a combination of two poisons that we can not live without. Oxygen is carried on the medium of nitrogen. Death gives room for new life to flourish. Good and evil, without which, there is no judgment. Our ugly brothers and sisters are sometimes our judges and protectors, artists and singers. Without the poor slaves, our arrogant wealthy would have no mansions. Honor all, and judge none, has been the message of the sages.

Through the standing stones, the human conscience has been expanded. The genetic changes will vibrate through the songs of Crescendjya. And the people will evolve in a healthy and balanced way, as long as there is even one Bluestone Standing.

THE END